SURVIVING JERSEY

DANGER & INSANITY IN THE GARDEN STATE

SCOTT LORING SANDERS

Outpost19 | San Francisco
outpost19.com

Sanders, Scott Loring
        Surviving Jersey: Danger & Insanity in The
Garden State / Scott Loring Sanders
        ISBN: 9781944853358 (pbk)

Library of Congress Control Number: 2017910727

This is a work of nonfiction. The events and experiences
described here are true to the author's memory. Only
a few names have been changed, as needed, when
individuals could not be reached for their permission.

OUTPOST19

ORIGINAL
PROVOCATIVE
READING

There is no rule that states I can't dedicate a second book to my parents. And even if there is such a rule, I'm breaking it. So, with that said:

For my mother and father, who raised me right, who always provided, and who loved me, unconditionally, through thick and thin. I thank you.

If you aren't gonna say exactly how you feel,
you might as well not say anything at all.
– Johnny Cash

In Jersey, anything's legal
as long as you don't get caught.
– Bob Dylan, from *Tweeter and the Monkey Man*

SURVIVING
JERSEY

DANGER & INSANITY
IN THE GARDEN STATE

BEFORE
JERSEY

MY FATHER

My father's name is Tommy Lee Sanders. That's the actual name printed on his birth certificate. He did his best to go by Tom for the majority of his adult life.

My father, in 1966, jumped off a third story hotel balcony with intentions of diving headfirst into a pool. The problem was, the supports were loose and gave way as he stood atop the iron railing and pushed off. He lost his purchase, couldn't soar out far enough. When he hit, he snapped both wrists on the pool's concrete edge. A fair amount of beer was involved. He flew off to Vietnam a week later. I've seen a picture of him in his olive drabs, his bright white casts standing out in stark contrast. I wasn't born yet, or even conceived. If he'd come-up just a few inches shorter, it's quite probable I wouldn't exist.

My father was born in Stuttgart, Arkansas in 1940, a land as level and flat as lake water, a land of levees and rice and soybeans. Stuttgart is the self-proclaimed rice and duck capital of the world. I once stayed in a hotel there. All of the hallways had rubber mats over the carpets (think car floor mats, but in extremely long strips) to catch all the mud from the hunters' boots after they came back from a long day of killing ducks. That's the town where my father was born.

My father was an Army brat. His father served in World

War II and Korea. My father went to a private, Catholic, all-boys, military high school in Alexandria, Louisiana. Think about that for a second: private, Catholic, all-boys, military. Menard High School. When I called him to ask how to spell it, he said: *Menard…Mike, Echo, November, Alpha, Romeo, Delta.*

My father was valedictorian of his class. Technically that's not true—there was a tie, so the principal flipped a coin and my father called heads when he should have called tails, so he got salutatorian. Things were different back then. The brothers (his teachers) wore black cassocks and draped crucifixes around their necks. There was a rumor that, at one time, the brothers would tie the arms of left-handed students behind their backs and make them compose with their right. The brothers would hit the boys if they so much as talked out of turn or looked out the window at a girl. The brothers used a tight fist to the back of the head. The brothers had a special room called "the snake pit," where they put the boys who didn't excel.

My father never stepped foot in a church after graduation, save for a wedding or funeral.

My father taught me right from wrong without ever raising a hand (though he raised his voice plenty.)

My father attended the U.S. Naval Academy, but didn't finish.

My father was an officer in Vietnam. With the Army.

My father has a BS from LSU and an MBA from Georgia State.

My father worked his ass off his entire adult life as an executive for AT&T in New Jersey.

My father was always embarrassed that his real name was Tommy Lee. He thought it made him sound like an ignorant country bumpkin. Ignorant country bumpkin he isn't.

My father is adamantly opposed to handguns. He's written many a vitriolic letter-to-the-editor expressing his hatred of the NRA. He's been a staunch defender of gay rights as far back as the 1970s. That's right: the 1970s. He's written many a letter to the editor about that, too. Same goes for civil rights.

My father's father was a flat-out racist.

My father's father once took me for a drive in Arkansas to show me "Niggertown."

My father's father once took me to a private club he belonged to. The Pam-Pam. You couldn't simply enter like you would at a normal restaurant; he had to knock on a door. There was a little panel in the solid wood that mysteriously slid open, and he had to say his name or some secret word. I don't remember which; I was just a boy. After giving the password, he turned to me and said, "That's to keep the niggers out." The Pam-Pam served delicious steaks and the best, fluffiest Arkansas rice I've ever tasted, smothered in butter. Most of the kitchen help was black.

My father's father went blind late in his life. He tried to step in front of a passing truck and kill himself near the end. He failed. I've never asked my father how that incident affected him.

My father's mother was legally blind in one eye from the time she was a little girl. She later went blind in her other eye, too. When she died, she had severe dementia. She didn't even know who my father was. I've never asked my father how that affected him, either.

My father, later in life, on vacation in Kiawah, South Carolina, took a little girl's pink foam pool noodle one evening. Then he walked across the backyard toward a canal: tepid, brackish, and filled with crabs, clams, and shrimp. That canal was also home to one menacing alligator, which had come up on shore. "Tom, get back here…Tom, you're scaring the children…Tom, you're drunk." My father, gripping the pink noodle, walked across the Bermuda grass toward the six foot gator (he claims ten foot gator, so I'm willing to meet him in the middle. Eight foot gator.) The little girl, a friend's granddaughter, began crying—whether out of fear and concern for my father or (more likely) for her noodle, I can't say. But she did cry. Perhaps someone might have advised—if anyone had known at the time, had happened to have such random stats filed away—that an alligator can run nearly ten miles per hour. My father, at 275 pounds, at sixty-something years old, with a bad back, could probably run four miles an hour. Maybe five if a gator was after him. Regardless, my father walked up to the animal, only a noodle's length away, and without hesitation, smacked the beast right across the top of its ridged snout. The alligator opened its jaws and held them ajar. So my father smacked the gator again, this time right in the mouth. That poor animal, still amazed by my father's audacity, only did what it's programmed to do. It snapped down on that helpless noodle, causing the ends to curl into a pink smile. And then it backpedaled into the murk of the canal and slowly submerged, the pink tips like periscopes as they disappeared beneath the surface. The little girl went into hysterics, suggesting that her concern had indeed been only for the noodle. My father was pleased with his bravado.

My father once drove by several bags of garbage on the side of the road. He pulled over, picked up the bags, opened them, and found discarded junk mail and letters, all with the same address. He put the trash in his trunk, found the presumed home, and planned to throw the bags on the front lawn. At the last moment, he decided against it because he couldn't be absolutely sure. To this day, he regrets that decision.

My father always loved that old commercial where the Indian cried by the highway while staring in anguish at all the litter.

My father had a pack of matches and, when I was six, asked me, "Have you ever seen a match burn twice?" I said that I hadn't. So he lit one and let it burn for a few seconds. Then he blew it out. "That's once, right?" he said. I nodded. Then he took the head of that hot match and stuck it to the bare skin of my arm. "That's twice," he said, and laughed. Don't have a hissy fit. It shocked me but didn't hurt. Not really. And I learned something important that day. Both about life and my father.

My father's appendix burst, and when the doctors did a standard biopsy following the operation to remove it, they found that he had colon cancer. He beat it.

My father, without telling anyone, parachuted out of an airplane to celebrate his sixtieth birthday, not too long after the colon cancer.

My father occasionally wears penny loafers with tube socks, khaki shorts, and a tucked-in white t-shirt—belt optional.

My father voted for George H.W. Bush.

My father voted for Bill Clinton. Twice.

My father voted for George W. Bush. Twice. Yes, even the second time. (The Swift Boater propaganda worked on my father. Don't mess with Vietnam vets; he takes that shit very personally.)

My father voted for Barack Obama. Twice.

My father voted for Hillary Clinton. He is sickened and disgusted by Donald Trump, has taken the outcome hard. He doesn't understand what's happened to the country he loves so much. The one he proudly risked his life for.

My father loves storms and lightning and thunder.

My father has witnessed two tornadoes. On both occasions, he stood outside and watched instead of seeking shelter.

My father is amazed by the stars, the moon, the planets, the space station, satellites.

My father, as a boy, busted apart thermometers so he

could play with the mercury. That might explain a lot, actually.

My father has exactly seven toothbrushes in his bathroom—one for each day of the week. I'm not joking. He has tried to explain his logic, something about how it makes each one last longer. It makes no goddamn sense.

My father once punished me for two weeks of summer vacation because I forgot to brush my teeth. I never forgot again.

My father was intimidating. Sometimes, even cruel. He could make me feel small and inadequate. I was never good enough. I always did things wrong. It took me a long time, well into adulthood, to realize that almost always when he acted that way, there was alcohol on his breath. As a teenager, I rebelled. I'd had enough. I drank and did drugs, got in trouble, had no ambition, no motivation, no purpose. I didn't care.

My father and I had a lot of long, hard, bitter years. We didn't like each other for quite a while. A lot of that was my fault. A lot of it was his.

My father taught me to stand up to bullies, not because they harassed me but because they bullied those who couldn't defend themselves. He said to get in their face just once and they'd back off and run away with their tails between their legs. He was right. I protected several kids when I was young, thanks to him, and I'm still proud of that. But I could never stand up to my father.

My father taught me honesty. To be a leader. My father

taught me the value of hard work, not by preaching it but by doing it. He taught me how to take care of my family, to raise my son, to do whatever I had to do to put food on the table. He taught me the importance of a firm handshake and to look the person in the eye when doing it. He taught me how to play poker. And never to welch on a bet.

My father pronounces *naked* as "nekid."

My father calls a gas station a "filling station."

My father eats cereal every morning with slices of banana. When he was a kid, he ate cereal with weevils crawling around in the grain. He still eats eggs well after their expiration date. Milk too. My father easily puts a quarter-stick of butter on one dinner roll. More if there's any surface area left.

My father drinks too much, eats too much, is overweight. But he's happy. And he's earned it.

My father let me drive for the first time when I was twelve. A little 1980 Honda hatchback. He let me lean over and steer while he worked the clutch, stick, gas, and brake. We were headed to McDonald's to pick up dinner. Oncoming cars made me nervous, but he didn't seem concerned. He trusted me. As we came off the bridge spanning the Musconetcong River in New Jersey, the traffic light turned yellow. My father punched it, but a car pulled out from our right, zipping from the Golden Skillet. There was no time to react. We slammed into the driver's side door. My knees went into the dashboard. The Honda's horn wouldn't stop blowing. My father grabbed the steering wheel and pulled violently. The horn stopped. The traffic stopped. The ache in my knees didn't stop. The cops were there even before my father exited to examine the damage. "Let's not tell anyone you were steering," he whispered, after making sure I was okay. I nodded as steam oozed from the crumpled hood. It was as close to a lie as I've ever heard him say. At least as far as I'm aware.

My father let me drive for real in Arkansas two years later. On flat, straight roads with only soybean fields in every direction, I sat behind the wheel and went for it. I got up to fifty-five miles per hour. My father even let me pass a car that was going too slow. In New Jersey, the driving age was seventeen. I drove for the first time three years before I could legally get my license. Technically, I got into my first car accident five years before I could legally get my license. But nobody knew that…except my father.

My father saw a woman pull out in front of a semi and get killed instantly. Her fault. My father was first on the scene. He was also first on the scene when a neighbor had a heart attack and crashed into a telephone pole. The neighbor died, too.

My father's eulogy will be given by me someday. This essay is what I'll read (if there is a eulogy, that is.) My father believes that once you're dead, that's it. No heaven, no hell, no nothing. He's made it emphatically clear that he doesn't want a ceremony after he dies. No service. No memorial. No fanfare. He wants to be cremated as cheaply as possible and then, The End. When my mother asked what we should do with his ashes, my father looked her dead in the eye, and, without missing a beat, said, "Surprise me."

My father taught me how to change a tire when I was fifteen.

My father pulled over and changed the tire of a stranded black woman during a pouring rainstorm. He was dressed in his suit and tie, and was late for work. But he did it.

My father and I swam with a pair of dolphins in the Bahamas. Not at some fancy resort, but out in the middle of the crystalline ocean, completely on our own, at sunset, with snorkel gear. One came directly at me, so close that I heard—or actually felt—the clicks it made with its jaw.

My father retired on a lake. The lake attracted Canada geese, which liked to use his lawn as their toilet. That pissed my father off. So he chased the flocks of geese with his Sea-Doo, sending them honking and flapping and racing over the water. Once, he did that with my five-year-old son sitting between his legs. Somehow he thought that was a good idea. The neighbors didn't agree and let him know about it. My father let them know he didn't give a rat's ass what they thought, nor did he care that "the geese were here first."

My father no longer has a problem with goose shit on his lawn.

My father told my son, ten years after the goose incident, that he didn't care for him much when he'd been a child. Said he'd been more or less a little shit.

My son loves my father a ton. Thinks he's hilarious. Calls him Granddaddy.

My father has never stolen as much as one penny in his entire life. If I was ever told otherwise, I'd truly be shocked.

My father once tied his dead, broken-down riding mower to the back of his Pontiac—the front wheels resting on the trunk of the car, the rear wheels on the pavement, the entire machine tilted at a forty-five-degree angle as if popping a wheelie—and towed it to the dump because he didn't want to pay to have someone haul it off.

My father has a lot of lawnmower stories. Here's another: his front yard is extremely steep. He likes to mow in the evening while drinking wine out of his favorite New Jersey Devils plastic cup. His wine cup. One day he came down the hill running a little hot, turned the wheels too sharply, and flipped the thing. He got tossed and when he looked up, a giant orange Husqvarna riding mower was barreling toward him, so he logrolled down the hill like a 275 pound child trying to get dizzy. He was sixty-four when he did that.

My father did the exact same thing a month later, except this time the damn mower did run him over. He bruised his ribs and messed up his elbow. When he examined himself in the mirror after the accident, he noticed black tread marks imbedded on his white T-shirt.

My father is unable to look in the mirror and see the scars that Vietnam left. But they're there. He lost one man under his command. I originally wanted to write,

He lost only *one man under his command,* but whether he'd lost one or one hundred, it was still too many for him. It affected/affects him profoundly. One of the hardest things I ever did was approach him and suggest that he go to a therapist who worked with Vietnam vets. He didn't want to go, didn't feel he needed any help, but he went for me.

My father has never cried in front of me.

My father took me to my first movie when I was five. It was the war film *Midway.* Not *Bambi* or *Snow White* or whatever children's movie happened to be playing, but *Midway.*

My father, when I was in first grade, showed me the giant, zipper-like scar he got after his hernia operation. He said, "That's where a shark bit me." I thought that was cool. I wanted a scar like that when I grew up.

My father was good at catching snakes. I thought that was cool, too.

My father, around the same time he showed me the hernia scar, let me play with his binoculars. He warned me never to look at the sun through them. As soon as he turned around and went back to his business, I took the binoculars and aimed them straight at the sun. I've never done that again.

My father, his mishap at the hotel pool notwithstanding, was an expert diver and an excellent swimmer. He taught me to do a backflip when I was three years old. We have pictures to prove it. Bystanders were amazed. He could also do a gainer. I never could.

My father's favorite movie is a tie between *Babe* and *Shrek*. His favorite song is "Bridge over Troubled Water." My father has his very own X-Box. The only game he plays is *Call of Duty*.

Up until I was nearly forty years old, I don't remember my father ever telling me he loved me. Now, often with drink on his breath (but not always), he tells me all the time.

THE SECOND PERSON

It's 1976 and you're living on the outskirts of Columbia, South Carolina. You're six years old. You don't see Dad much because he's always working. He has a job with AT&T, something involving towers and cables. He travels a lot, to Atlanta and other big cities, so mostly it's just you and Mom. She teaches you to read from a book about a dog named Pug. She takes you to Hardee's a few days a week, and you play on the ginormous outdoor jungle gym after you eat. She teaches you the Bump and you dance with her in the den, spinning 45s on your record player. Songs like "Boogie Fever" and "Disco Duck" and "Play That Funky Music." But in your own room you are obsessed with KISS, and you listen to the *Destroyer* album over and over, especially "Detroit Rock City" because it tells a story. Ace's solo is so sad and mournful—even at six, you understand how that weeping guitar sets the tone for the main character's impending death. Mom doesn't appreciate KISS the way you do, though she concedes "Beth" is a pretty song.

When you're upstairs in your room, you go to a different place as the music plays on the cheap plastic turntable. There's you—the physical you sitting on the bed—but then there's that second you, floating above and watching the story unfold as Paul Stanley advises to *get up and move your feet*. This second person watches the tragic ballad playout as you—the tangible you—stares at your bottle collection while wearing your favorite

14

red t-shirt with KISS emblazoned across the chest, the letters silver and sparkly, the two S's not actually S's at all, but cool lightning bolts instead. Those two S's are also your initials, which, in your young mind, stirs some sort of illogical kinship.

Other than a few news clips about the KISS phenomena sweeping the country, and browsing through music magazines at the Piggly Wiggly, your access to images of the band is limited. You remember that one magazine had Paul Stanley on the cover licking a Popsicle. "KISS REVEALED" is to the side of him, a major story because nobody knows their true identities. Only recently has your six-year-old mind started to comprehend that each band member leads two lives. There's Peter, Paul, Ace, and Gene in full regalia, of course. But each of them is also a second person, a real person, sans makeup and seven-inch high-heeled boots adorned with fiery-eyed dragon heads. So when you open that magazine to get a glimpse of the faces behind the makeup, you receive your first lesson in bait-and-switch. That "exclusive" photo is a sham. All it shows is a long-haired man with his hands over his face (as if crying or ashamed), rushing from a limo to a hotel entrance. That long-haired man could be anyone, though the caption claims it's Paul Stanley. You are disappointed. But also relieved, you realize, because in reality you don't want the mystique to unravel, for the game to be spoiled.

•

You're happy Dad's coming home. You love him and

15

can't wait to see him, but what you're really eager for is the surprise he'll bring. Because he always brings a surprise. You know *what* it will be, you just don't know the variety yet. When he shows up that evening in his suit and tie, you greet him by hugging his leg. After a few brief formalities, he reaches inside his jacket and produces not one, not two, but four miniature liquor bottles. You're ecstatic because they're a brand you don't have: J&B Scotch. You race to your room to place the empties on your windowsill alongside the others: Jack Daniels, Smirnoff, Cutty Sark. You unscrew one of the red J&B caps and take a sniff. The odor is sharp but comforting, reminds you of Dad.

Dad is Superman. You once watched him fly off your roof, and as he landed, he dropped his shoulder and tucked into a roll before popping back up—*ta-da*—unharmed, exhibiting the soldier techniques he used in Vietnam. In the morning, you will play catch with him. You are already a gifted baseball player, and he recognizes this. He enjoys making the occasional bad toss, just to test your athletic prowess. He is your world and can do no wrong...until he starts drinking from larger replicas of those airplane bottles. If he consumes enough, he becomes a second person. Different from the man who pitches you a bucket of balls in the backyard. He's never violent, but there's a sharp edge to his tongue, usually directed at Mom. But sometimes he fires at you, points out your inadequacies. This makes you sad, but he's your dad, so you forgive him.

Arguments rise from downstairs when you're supposed to be sleeping. Sometimes you hear Mom crying. You don't correlate the liquor bottles with that second Dad until you're a little older. But not much older, really. It's not that hard to figure out. You don't understand the complexities of alcohol or depression or PTSD, so you keep it simple: when he drinks, he can be fun and unrestrained. Other times, nasty and demeaning.

It takes you forty years to realize that the first time he gave you an airplane bottle, it was most likely by accident. He'd probably forgotten to stop at the airport gift shop, so he thought quickly on his feet when you inquired about your surprise. He desperately patted his pants pockets, then his jacket pockets, searching for something, anything, to conjure into a present. That's when he produced the miniature liquor bottle. He pitched its importance like it was a valuable treasure. And you bought it, hook, line, and sinker, admiring the black-and-white label with *Old No. 7* printed in fancy lettering. He was smooth, your dad, just like that Tennessee whiskey.

•

Two brothers, Chad and Brad, live in your neighborhood. Less than a year apart, they are your gateway into the larger world. They teach you how to pull cats' tails. They teach you the word *Fuck*. And also *Nigger*. Similar to how you don't understand Dad's drinking, you don't yet fully comprehend those words or their greater meanings.

At the creek, you catch tadpoles and crawdads with Chad and Brad. Or you throw beer bottles, soda cans, and sticks upstream, then bomb the hell out of the Japanese Navy as the armada drifts toward you. When one of your large rocks obliterates a ship, you yell "We hit the Jap-pot!," mimicking a line from the film *Midway*, which Dad took you to see a few weeks before, not because it was appropriate for a six-year-old, but because he was a World War II junkie and Mom put him in charge that day. As reticent as he was about Vietnam, he's effusive about World War II, an aficionado, teaches you all there is to know. He creates a homemade version of the game Battleship, and the two of you play for hours, searching out the others destroyers and subs.

Across the creek is an open, weedy field. Beyond that, at the edge of a pine wood, a shantytown. Five hundred feet from your middleclass neighborhood, with its two-story houses, concrete driveways, with bicycles and skateboards and baseballs and basketballs strewn about, are weathered gray shacks the color of fruit mold. Stovepipes poke through tin roofs scabbed with rust. Clotheslines hold ghostly effeminate shapes that bounce and sway in the breeze. It's an entirely different world. A forbidden world, even though you don't ever recall being told it was forbidden. That was simply understood.

One day while at the creek, a couple of black kids appear on the opposite bank. You and Chad and Brad stop your bombing and stare at them. They do the same. It's a stream maybe ten feet wide, but it might as well be a raging river dividing countries. You don't recall any exchange of words or explanation, but your game wasn't exactly rocket science to begin with. You and Chad and Brad toss some sticks and cans upstream, then collect rocks and fire away. The black boys join in and it's great fun until those ships float directly in front of the two opposing sides. You sling your rocks, they sling theirs, all with similar good intentions of sinking the fleet, but you aren't old enough, don't have the foresight yet, to see that some of your rocks will careen across, that splashes might cause the other guys to get wet, or worse, get hit by a stray rock. Your fake war turns into a real one, your bombs and torpedoes now redirected. Things escalate until the black boys turn tail and run back to their shantytown mommies. "Hit the niggers, hit the niggers," yell Chad and Brad, lofting long shots at the fleeing enemy. Only minutes before, you'd been little boys doing little boy things. Then suddenly it's all different.

It's 1976. You're six years old. You can't yet comprehend social classes, economic disparity, racism. You live in the same town as the black boys—the same neighborhood, really. Only a small creek divides your family from theirs. But the geographical barrier isn't what causes the true division. Your family isn't wealthy or poor, just solid middleclass. But them? They live on the fringes of that field, on the fringes of society. They exist in the squalid conditions of a Third World country as second-class citizens.

Afterward, you proudly tell your mother about the incident and how you *sent the niggers packin'*. She is taken aback, then collects herself and explains why you will *NEVER* use that word again. Your mother grew up in rural, poverty-stricken Central Alabama during the 1940s and '50s. She's seen some shit. So she teaches her first-grader, as best she can, about racism, injustice, and some of the world's cruelties.

It's a lesson that sticks.

•

You were playing in the woods with your next-door neighbor Elizabeth on a cold winter's afternoon. You stumbled upon two teenaged boys who offered you a dollar to run across a trampoline-sized patch of leaves and pine needles. It seemed simple enough: sprint from one end to the other, maybe ten strides. But that's when You stepped in. Something seemed off to You. Maybe it was the way the boys lipped their cigarettes, the butts hanging at the corners of their sneaky smiles. Maybe it was how they seemed all too eager to forfeit a dollar for such an effortless task. For whatever reason, You intervened and said, "No." It's the first recollection of You coming to the rescue.

But Elizabeth's second person wasn't as intuitive, and she eagerly agreed. The conniving boys counted down. *Three.* Elizabeth was all smiles. *Two.* She envisioned the Pixy Stix she'd buy. *One.* She could hardly stand it. *Go.* Elizabeth shot from the runner's blocks and travelled only two full steps before the swamp water swallowed her. She submerged completely before surfacing, her dark, stringy hair even more dark and stringy as it molded to her cheeks. The water was cold and she *gasped, gasped, gasped* to catch her breath. That little bog had been perfectly camouflaged, yet somehow You had sensed it.

The boys laughed, then took off without helping… or paying up. By now Elizabeth was crying, probably more from humiliation than the icy water itself. You walked her home, feeling empathy while simultaneously gloating. You hadn't fallen for it. She had.

So maybe that little incident was a godsend. Maybe you learned something that day about trust. And bullies. And bad people. And also about your inner You. Maybe that's why you are prepared for the molester kid when he finds you and your friend Kevin at the construction site. You like to scavenge around the new houses in the evenings when the workers are gone. In addition to collecting Dad's airplane bottles, you also collect soda bottles. They're worth a nickel apiece at the corner store where you proudly trade them in for cold hard cash to spend on candy and Wacky Pack stickers.

You scour the bare ground, looking for tall, slender bottles that have a heft to them. Solid and durable, like weapons. You love scoring 7Up or Sprite because they are dark green—not Coca-Cola blueish-green, not transparent like Nu-Grape or Pepsi—but a deep emerald. You enjoy how everything distorts when you examine the world through those tinted bottles, a pirate scanning the horizon with his telescope.

But business is slow this day. All you find are some stubby Pabst Blue Ribbons, a few Miller High Lifes. The problem with beer bottles is they're worthless. Made of cheaper, thinner glass, they're only good for one thing. Breaking. You set them up on stacks of 2x4's, or slide their mouths over the tips of low hanging pine branches. You create a shooting gallery, where the bottles are the Japs (always the poor Japs, never the Krauts for some reason) and you and Kevin, with your piles of rocks, are the Americans, flying your Corsairs as you blast the shit out of the Zeros. A full-on dogfight.

You know your father will be highly disappointed, breaking glass and leaving it scattered across the construction site. But your father isn't there, now is he? Off on another business trip, as usual. So it progresses, the breaking of the bottles. Mostly your shots are glancing, sending *clinks* across the grounds, but occasionally you score a direct hit, exploding a plane to bits. You again use your favorite line, "We hit the Jap-pot!" So the Zeros are falling like bugs in a zapper when you hear the words that stop you cold, that send hot spikes flashing up your spine. "What the hell do y'all think you're doing?"

A teenager you've never seen before, ball cap and long sloppy hair filtering down from the sides. Sick, rheumy eyes.

"Y'all know better than to bust bottles. That's bad. Really bad."

You stare at your sneakers, ashamed, and presume Kevin does the same. You've got a knot in your gut because you're busted. Heat prickles your cheeks as if being tattooed, and you fear molester kid will chaperone you to your house, force you to confess to your mother. But molester kid has different ideas.

"Y'all got anything to say for yourselves?" he says in a nasty sort of way, his sick little eyes bearing down on you, most likely mimicking the words and actions of his abusive father.

You shake your head, mumble, "No, sir," because that's how you've been taught to speak to your elders. *Yes, ma'am. No, sir.* Even though he's not an adult, you figure that right then isn't the best time to test the boundaries of etiquette.

"Both of y'all, inside, goddamnit," he says, nodding toward the unfinished house. A pair of 2x8s lie side-by-side at a forty-five degree incline, a makeshift ramp to the front door threshold. You go first, then Kevin. You can tell when molester kid follows because the boards bow and bounce, creating a wobbly effect, like trying to traverse a waterbed. Like walking the plank. You enter the gloom, notice the odor of sawdust and stale beer. Bent nails and sharp pieces of discarded flashing lie in wait across the plywood floors.

"Upstairs," says molester kid. "Gonna teach y'all a lesson."

You feel Kevin behind you as you approach the unfinished steps. Steps so incomplete that as you climb, you can see between each one, can see the first floor you're leaving behind. You want to call for Mom but know she can't hear you.

"In there," says molester kid, pointing toward a bedroom. This room seems a bit more finished. There's a built-in closet, sliding doors have been hung.

Tears well but you suppress them. Kevin isn't quite as successful. He whimpers. Molester kid senses weakness. "Get in that goddamn closet," he says to Kevin. He's not yelling, but his tone slices through you. His intentions, you now know for absolute certain, are not good. "I'll give you something to cry about," he says. His father's words again. Or a sketchy uncle's. Or a trusted family friend's. "Get in there."

Kevin slides the door open, enters the darkness. Molester kid follows but turns to you before he disappears. "Stay right there. Don't fucking move."

You obey, things blurry now, unable to suppress

your tears, though you did manage to hold out one minute longer than Kevin. As it so happens, that one little minute makes all the difference. From behind the closed door you hear, "Pull down your shorts." And that's when You take over. You don't care about molester kid's threats. You disobey. You're getting out. You're not stopping until you're in Mom's arms.

But you do stop once you're up the dirt road. Your neighbor is in his yard, an older man, push-mowing his front lawn. His home is directly across from yours. You realize you need to tell someone quickly because things are happening to Kevin. Bad things.

You startle the man, but he must see your panic and fear because he kills the mower and bends to your level. He lightly puts his hands on your shoulders, nods, asks you things you don't remember anymore.

And that's where it ends for you. The memories are gone, except that your mother is instantly there, it seems, as well as other neighborhood adults. You believe some of the men head toward the houses under construction, but you aren't positive of this.

You never see Kevin again. You move to New Jersey shortly thereafter. But forty years later, you still think about him occasionally. What would have become of you if Kevin hadn't been there to take the fall? What if you'd been alone while breaking bottles?

But you weren't. You had Kevin with you, that second person, who molester kid chose instead. Yet you can't help but think: How much different might your life be if not for him? How close had you come to being severely traumatized?

Pretty damn close, you imagine.

•

You have a second person living inside you, your go-to consultant, the person who helps you reason. You work as a team to make sense of the world. Your second person has saved you countless times, so it's hard to imagine people out there who can't trust theirs. But it's a fragile balance, this second person stuff, where the scales can easily tip either way.

There's also a fair amount of luck involved with maintaining a reliable second person. For example, some people, perhaps, *did* have the misfortune of being alone around a construction site when a molester kid happened by. Or maybe their fathers, after drinking too much, *did indeed* get violent. You recognize you've narrowly escaped what could have otherwise been an entirely different life. A traumatized life.

•

You're on the baseball field, proudly dressed in your uniform for picture day, disappointed that Dad is out of town again. Then panic ensues. You forgot your hat in the car. You run to Mom, frantic. She says, "I won't let them take the picture without you. Just go to the parking lot and get it." Mom eases your fears as usual. You happily sprint from the field and bound up the long set of concrete steps with the iron handrail in the middle. The car is unlocked and you struggle with the giant door's heft. It's a '71 Impala, a beast. It's the same vehicle that ten years later, in New Jersey, your father will gift to you as your first car. His pride and joy. He'd named it Betsy. It's the same vehicle that, only a few months later, you'll total because your friend challenged you, said he could drive that twisty mountain road faster. You accepted his challenge and made it nearly to the bottom when you overshot a sharp curve and smashed head-on into a van, catapulting that innocent driver into the back where he was rendered unconscious. Your chest and arms folded the steering wheel like melted plastic. Your friend's head shattered the windshield. Blood poured down his face, straight over his right eye and mouth. And that's when you freaked out, went into shock.

But on this day you have no way of knowing what future gore awaits you ten years down the road. No, on this day you're a happy little boy who grabs his hat, excited for team pictures. You make it halfway down the steps when suddenly somebody blocks your path. You look up, ready to politely say *excuse me,* when your stomach drops. Because there he is, molester kid, standing in front of you. There's a blankness in his sickly eyes that conveys he doesn't recognize you from the month before. But you sure as hell recognize him.

"Give me your hat," he says. You comply as your heart punches your face. He unsnaps the adjustable plastic band, re-snaps it around the iron railing, then flicks his wrist and sends your hat zooming down that rail as if part of a zip line. You bolt, not even bothering to grab your hat after you descend the steps. You find Mom and try to explain. She sees your genuine fear. A few minutes later, she returns with your hat but molester kid has vanished once more.

You get your team picture taken shortly thereafter,

and forty years later that 5x7 is still in one of your mom's albums. You look happy in the photo, innocent and excited. But that's not really you. In reality, as the photographer chimed, "'Say Cheese," you were breathing heavily, scanning the shadows of that parking lot on the hill, scared shitless for what you knew was out there. And always would be.

MY GRANDMOTHER, THE ORIGINAL QUEEN OF DEATH METAL

I blame my grandmother for my fascination with the dark side. Granny was a bit of an odd duck. Not exactly "grandmotherly." She wasn't loving or doting. Never asked me questions or played games. She didn't cook, didn't spoil her only grandson. Usually, she just sat in the den listening to television. I say "listening" because Granny was blind. When she'd been a little girl in 1920s Arkansas, a boy reared back and zinged an unripe persimmon at her head. The hard little fruit nailed her in the eye, detaching her retina. By the time I'd come along, fifty years later, the vision in her functioning eye had also failed. Macular degeneration, cataracts.

I only recall a few details about Granny.

One, most evenings she'd give me a Ring-Ding: a chocolate-covered, hockey-puck, marshmallow-stuffed cake. Each Ring-Ding was individually wrapped in aluminum foil (or maybe it was still tin foil back then?) and every time I unraveled one, it was like discovering a new treasure.

Two, she had a fluffy Pomeranian named Puddin who'd sit at her feet while she rocked in her chair. Granny kept her legs crossed, ladylike, and with her dangling foot, she'd rub Puddin's chin.

Three, after Granny ate ice cream, she allowed Puddin to lick the bowl, the spoon clinking the sides.

So that's what I recollect about her. And now that I think about it, two of those three memories were really more about Puddin. But I have one other. One which I've always found curious.

In the mid-1970s, when I was four or five, I sometimes stayed with Granny when my parents were away. In the mornings, we'd sit outside on her porch-swing in the sweltering Louisiana summers. She wore thick cat's-eye glasses with a black plastic insert behind the lenses, similar to what an optometrist distributes after dilation.

While we rocked, I'd watch birds flitter in the birdbath beneath a live oak, curtains of gray Spanish moss hanging from the limbs like wiry witch hair. And I'd listen as Granny sang one particular song, over and over. Her voice was soft, pleasant, and as we swayed it soothed me. But at some point I started paying attention to the words, put two-and-two together. The result was genuine fear.

The song was loosely based on a true story, of a father taking his daughters into the Pennsylvania woods and shooting them. *That* was the inspiration for the only song Granny ever sang to me. I don't know what she was thinking, don't know if she ever once considered the lyrics, but *I* sure as hell considered them, hiding beneath the covers in her guest room, all alone, late at night.

> *O my dears, don't you know*
> *How so very long ago*
> *Two little children*
> *Whose names I don't know*

Were stolen away
On a bright summer day
And left in the woods
So I've heard people say

When came the night
So sad was their plight
The sun went down
And the moon gave no light
They sobbed and they sighed
And they bitterly cried
Until the poor little babes
They lay down and died

And when they were dead
The robins so red
Brought strawberry leaves
And over them spread
And all the day long
They sang this sweet song
Poor babes in the woods
Poor babes in the woods

Thanks for that, Granny. Pretty uplifting stuff to sing to your grandson shortly after his parents abandoned him to go gallivanting in San Francisco. No problem, Mom, I'll be okay chillin' with Granny and her dark obsessions. No seriously, Dad, what's more comforting than a jam session with my morbid grandmother? You guys go walk the fucking Golden Gate or eat Chinese or whatever the hell. I'm four years old. I'll be fine.

Of course I *was* fine, and today, as a writer of

mystery and crime fiction, I believe I owe Granny some much deserved posthumous gratitude. Perhaps her terrifying song had been imprinted on my young brain, creating a lifelong fascination with stories of violence and darkness. So thanks, Granny, for sharing that gruesome dirge. Perhaps it shaped me into the man and writer I am today.

You didn't bother singing *You Are My Sunshine* to this tough little bastard. No sirree, Bob. A duet of *Eensy Teensy Spider* wasn't necessary in my formative years. You were all nature, no nurture. You went through the Depression. You single-handedly raised two children on military bases while your husband was off killing the Japanese, and later the Koreans. You were blind. A total badass.

So here's your fifteen minutes. The spotlight's on you. Rock it, Granny. Rock it hard.

SURVIVING
JERSEY

CIRCUS PRAYER

DEAR LORD,

THANK YOU FOR LETTING ME SURVIVE THE SEEDY and derelict circus that showed up on the ball fields of my New Jersey elementary school in 1979. If You recall, there were two shows: the early and the late, and I went to the former. I remember the pair of tigers sitting on pedestals with metal collars, the O-rings at the ends of their heavy chains affixed to steel spikes driven into the outfield. There was no fence or wall between the tigers and the incoming circus-goers. There was no cage of any sort. No, Dear Lord, the only dividers were landscaping timbers resting horizontally on cinderblocks, not more than a foot off the ground. A single line of those timbers created the only "barrier" as the patrons streamed into the tent. But anyone, from an adult to a toddler, could have easily stepped over and walked right up to a tiger if they had had the *cojones*. Could have easily, if so inclined, slapped one of the beasts across its beautiful whiskered face.

It was at the late show where all the excitement happened. But I wasn't at that show, Dear Lord. No, for whatever reason, You found it in my best interest to go to the early one. And I remember that after the incident, as a nine-year-old, I was angry with You. Not because You let the tragedy happen. No, instead I was angry (and also jealous) because I wasn't there to witness it while

35

many of my friends were. You chose to have me at home as that tiger leapt off its pedestal with just enough play in its chain to pounce on the boy, a boy my age from the next town over, who had strayed to the wrong side of that useless little barrier. Who had his neck bitten, mauled, and eaten by a three hundred? four hundred? five hundred? pound tiger. Who was killed by that tiger in front of a tent-full of onlookers. Who was pulled from the jaws of the beast by our school's custodian, Mr. Van Sulkama, albeit, a tad too late. And assisted by Mr. Borth, the father of one of my classmates.

The following day, Dear Lord, the circus had fled. But at recess I, along with a girl from my class, found a bloody, goopy pile of something in the grass near third base. Something the size and color of a juvenile eggplant. A deep purple that resembled smashed poke berries. Thirty years later, after I located the girl on Facebook, I asked if she remembered that goopy pile or was it something my young mind had invented. She remembered.

And the parents Lord, oh, the parents. Two sets in this instance. Because You didn't have the boy go with his own parents, no, but with the parents of a friend. So *they* were responsible for the boy's wellbeing. How does one live with that sort of guilt for the rest of his or her life?

And here's an update, Lord, nearly forty years later. I've since learned I was wrong about the boy going with a different set of parents. Instead, it was far worse. He went with his babysitter. And she hadn't gotten permission, just took the boy along because she wanted to see her friends. And after the incident—but before the true horror was fully understood, when the scene was still pure chaos—friends of mine overheard her saying, "Do you think he'll be okay? I'm probably going to get in big trouble for this."

Trouble indeed, Lord. What sort of life did You let her lead from that day forward?

And then the actual parents of the boy, Lord. They go out to dinner or a movie or just to have a little alone time. They leave their son at home with a presumably mature, trustworthy young girl from the neighborhood. Perhaps a friend's daughter, or maybe recommended by one of the women from bridge club. Who knows? And then those parents return home, refreshed and happy after a few hours to themselves. But upon entering the front door, the first thing they notice is how quiet it is. It seems odd. Then they realize the babysitter isn't there. Nor is their son. How quickly do they figure things out from there, Lord? Who exactly informs them of their child's fate? Not kidnapped, not killed in a car accident, but eaten by a tiger. How many parents, in the history of all parents in civilization, can say their child was killed in such a way? A hundred maybe? Ever? And at least if it was in India or wherever tigers still roam, at least then the parents could make some sort of sense of it. Still painful, yes, but it could be rationalized. But in New Jersey, Lord? How do the parents begin to make heads or tails of that one? How awkward must that conversation be, even forty years later, when new acquaintances ask innocent questions about family, maybe while at a dinner party and they see an old photo of the boy on the wall? "Oh, who is that handsome little guy?" And then the mother, or maybe the father, tries to explain. Why would You do that to those poor parents? Were they atheists or something? Had they denounced Your name at some point way back when?

Is it bad, Dear Lord, that I wanted to be there that night? To see that boy ripped open and partially eaten by a tiger? Why did You spare me that, yet, in Your infinite wisdom, allow me outside for recess the very next day to find the boy's viscera lying in the hot sunshine beneath a swarm of hungry green-bottle flies? To let my imagination run wild with disturbing visions possibly more horrific than if I'd just witnessed the actual event? I know I'm not supposed to question the whys of Your ways, Dear Lord, but I'm asking anyway because quite frankly, it doesn't make a whole lot of damn sense. No sense that I can see anyway. As You well know, I'm not much on praying, so I'm not sure about etiquette here. How does the prayer stop? Do I thank you? Do I cross myself or leave some offering? Or do I just end it, and hope that somehow You'll reply?

WHERE YOU CONTROL
THE ACTION

The most insane waterpark ever created was located in a small town in northern New Jersey: Action Park. Action Park was like the Wild, Wild West of waterparks, except instead of guns and saloons and prostitutes, there were water rides and wave pools and alpine slides with little-to-no supervision. Action Park didn't really have rules; laws didn't exist within its boundaries. There were no strict or significant safety measures in place, at least none adhered to. It's been referred to as The Most Dangerous Waterpark in the World, a moniker the owner and founder, Gene Mulvihill, was apparently proud of. From 1980-1987, there were six confirmed fatalities—from drownings to electrocutions to head traumas, along with hundreds (if not thousands) of annual injuries.

How Action Park ever opened in the first place is still a mystery. How it was allowed to *remain* open is an even bigger one. The grounds were home to a ski resort in the winter and a waterpark in the summer. Teenagers openly drank beer and smoked inside the park, and many of those were *employees*. As a preteen, I was far more scared of the clientele than I was of the rides themselves, worried I might get picked on or ostracized or beaten up. But as a teenager, it was one of the greatest, wildest, craziest places on Earth. If the film *Caddyshack* had been set at a waterpark instead of a golf course, that might offer a glimpse of what it was like. Except Action Park wasn't fiction, Action Park was real.

The park was composed of countless death-defying rides, the majority of which would be illegal today. Part of the reason they were so dangerous was because the patrons were in control of their own fate. Action Park's motto was, "Where *you* control the action." Imagine giving teenagers free rein to do whatever they wanted, and then hire another set of teenagers to operate the rides. The result? Potential disaster mixed with extreme and unlimited fun. For example, the Tarzan Swing was the equivalent of any classic rope swing. It was a long waterskiing rope attached to a horizontal post (a gallows might be a fair comparison) where participants swung out and dropped twenty feet into a freezing, spring-fed pond (one of the confirmed deaths occurred when a man had a heart attack after plunging into the frigid water.) If a person on the Tarzan Swing panicked—which happened often—and didn't let go, there was no safeguard preventing them from swinging back and slamming into the platform. Others slipped or didn't have the upper body strength to hold on until they reached the apex. These mistakes often resulted in face-plants or belly-flops.

But the physical repercussions of a mishap were nothing compared to the mental. It was commonplace for spectators on the boardwalk to surround the Tarzan Swing with the sole intention of loudly mocking those who had accidents. Their only job was to offer scorching ridicule. And it didn't matter how old the swinger was. The crowd was as ruthless to a ten-year-old girl as they were to a twenty-something man. As a young kid, it was terrifying. I was once there with a friend who was overweight, one of those guys who always wore a t-shirt when swimming to mask his belly fat. His hands slipped off the handle shortly into his descent, and he scraped against the wooden platform before awkwardly tumbling into the pond, ass-over-head. The crowd went nuts, screaming fat slurs. He'd only been twelve years old, but no one offered mercy. No one really gave a damn. He broke down in tears, humiliated, and I felt horrible for him. But I had to suck it up quickly, as I was next in line.

Another ride was the Cannonball, essentially a padded sewer pipe. Halfway through the tunneled slide, the pipe elbowed forty-five degrees. The water source was provided by a garden hose that had to be stepped over before entering the dark maw. That was the level of sophistication at Action Park—a garden hose. The drunk or stoned operator would say "Go ahead" and off you'd shoot. If you wanted to go backwards, the operator didn't care. Tandem? No problem, dude. There was no mat or carpet or other riding device; it was just you, sliding down the steep decline of a pitch-black tube, having no idea when you'd hit that elbow. Once there, you'd pinball side-to-side before seeing the light at the end of the tunnel, literally. When you reached that light, you'd be launched through the air until you landed in another freezing pond. No chlorine in that water, by the way. No safeguards against bacteria or urine. No nothing. Just a frigid pond you might land in feet first, face first, belly first, or back first. I don't recall a lifeguard on duty. There must've been, but I was far more concerned with the jeering crowds than I was with drowning.

Perhaps the most dangerous ride of all was the Cannonball Loop. Extraordinarily short-lived, it had the same premise as the Cannonball, except there was a 360 degree loop at the end, similar to a rollercoaster. But while a rollercoaster used chains and tracks and electrical power to thrust patrons upside down and around, the Cannonball Loop depended on nothing more than the weight of a rider's body and centrifugal force. In other words, it was virtually impossible. The ride only lasted a month because people kept smashing their faces, breaking their noses, and injuring their backs. One rumor claimed that when the Cannonball Loop was first constructed, homemade dummies were thrust down the tube, emerging from the other end dismembered or decapitated. Later, employees were offered a hundred dollars by Mr. Mulvihill if they'd test ride it. Again, that was the level of sophistication at Action Park. Their methods weren't much more advanced than how my friends and I used to build bike ramps in the neighborhood, using loose stacks of bricks and flimsy plywood. It was easy to imagine the "architects" of these rides as nothing more than a bunch of drunk guys sitting around a table, brainstorming while they got wasted.

"Dude, what if we made a waterslide that did a loopty-loop?"

"Oh, man, that would be fucking awesome."

So they built it, what the hell, with no knowledge of physics, engineering, or apparent regard for human life.

Another attraction was the Wave Pool, one of the

first of its kind, which was always filled with white kids and black kids and brown kids and yellow kids. Kids from rural Jersey, inner-city Jersey, from Brooklyn and the Bronx, all packed into a calm, giant swimming pool that slowly started moving. And then the waves would grow larger and stronger until kids bobbed in water that resembled a churning ocean. It was a manmade tsunami, where visitors were slammed and tossed into each other like lottery balls. Those who attempted to escape by climbing out the sides usually didn't fare well. They'd be pounded into the concrete walls, then sucked back into the water like buoys in an unforgiving tide. On its inaugural day, the waves were so strong and lasted so long that more than one hundred people had to be rescued. The Wave Pool was responsible for more deaths than any other attraction in the park.

The most infamous ride of all was the Alpine Slide, which wasn't even a water ride. Its concrete track, similar to a luge, wound its way down the side of the ski slope. Park goers had to take a chair lift to the top of the mountain to get there. No helmets, no gloves, no knee or elbow pads. I don't even think shoes were required. A longhaired teenager often wearing a *Black Sabbath* or *Yes* concert T, with a cigarette hanging from his lips, distributed plastic sleds with steel wheels. The only means for braking was a rudimentary handle that poked between the legs (a potential disaster for boys) and when pulled back on, scraped against the concrete. In other words, the rider was in charge of his speed, following Action Park's core principle. The Black Sabbath guy didn't have a walkie-talkie to coordinate with the operator at the bottom, and there were no spotters at various points to make sure the flume was free and clear. If somebody crashed half-way down and was stuck on the track, there was no way to know. Collisions with fellow riders were inevitable.

Two separate tracks ran next to one another, snaking down the hillside like parallel mountain streams. When it was your turn, you scooted to the edge until gravity took over. And then you were off, screaming down the side of the mountain with no one in control of your destiny except you. It was total freedom, as exhilarating as it was frightening. People sometimes flew off the tracks and into the weeds if they entered a turn too hot. There were no pads or cages or nets. If you went too fast, you risked serious injury or death. The first documented fatality at Action Park was a nineteen-year-old employee who hit his head on the surrounding rocks after being tossed.

Think about all of that for a moment—you are a teenager on a tiny cart ripping down the side of a mountain with nothing to regulate your speed. You have a teenager's brain, a teenager's reasoning, and a teenager's inhibitions. Or lack thereof. You are allowed to go as fast as you damn well please. *That* was an actual ride at Action Park.

Scrapes and cuts were commonplace. People finished the Alpine Slide bleeding, the result of bare skin skidding across rough concrete at twenty miles per hour. You often saw friends at school or a party with friction burns on their knees or elbows. If you asked what happened and they replied, "Alpine Slide," no further questioning was necessary. Everyone in Jersey knew what that meant. The wounds and scars were worn like badges of honor.

Action Park was debauchery at its finest. I know it probably seems like I'm exaggerating. It sounds like one of those instances where the myth, over time, tends to outgrow the reality. But Action Park was not a myth. Or exaggeration. It was a real place, and real people got injured and even died there. It shut down in 1996 although a safer, tamer version recently opened, called Mountain Creek. Of course, because of safety regulations and our ever-growing litigious society, it will never be the same as the original. Which is probably a good thing, at least if the preservation of life is important to you.

And I need to be clear about something. As scary and dangerous as Action Park was, it was also amazing. Where you could be as hedonistic as you wanted without fear of repercussions (other than severe bodily injury, of course). Gene Mulvihill was way ahead of his time. He created something unlike any other place on earth. During that small window of history when Action Park existed, my friends and I took full advantage. We were lucky enough to experience true and glorious freedom. No rules. No authority. No restraints. Just running amok in Jersey, raw and wild.

COLD-BLOODED LOVE

On a chilly October afternoon in 1977, my father and I talked as we hiked along the banks of the Musconetcong River, discussing the impending birth of my first sibling. Since Mom was due in a few days, Dad described how things would change. At seven years old, I'd gotten accustomed to being an only child and wasn't eager to relinquish that title. If I had to have a sibling, I would've much preferred acquiring a big brother versus becoming one.

As Dad explained his expectations—do my chores without being told, pick up after myself, clear my dinner plate, be a good little soldier—I spied a rope swing hanging from a mottled sycamore, a fat knot tied in the bottom, swaying back-and-forth like a lazy pendulum. As I approached, I had trouble grasping it, both for its girth as well as a slimy glaze covering the fibers. Dad continued lecturing, but I'd had enough "responsibility" talk. I wanted to plant my sneakers on that knotted foothold and sail over the river, challenging and mocking the cold water below before returning safely to the bank.

It had been a windy, rainy fall, so most of the trees were leafless. Crusty balls of foam collected in various eddies in the smaller weirs while whitewater raced over the rocks upstream. The air chilled me as it rose off the surface, misting my face. It was only mid-October, but a rawness had already settled in.

"Can I swing out?" I asked, knowing I'd be denied.

Dad considered the rope, then the swift, undulating water before conceding. "You better hold on tight. That water looks cold."

I hadn't expected consent, so suddenly I wasn't sure I wanted to go through with it. The idea had been enticing—and safe—when I knew I wouldn't be allowed, but now with permission granted, the appeal diminished.

"Really?" I asked.

"Sure, but hold on like your life depended on it."

My father was an imposing man: six feet, two hundred pounds, strong jaw line, solid military muscle. Years later, my friends were often scared to visit my house. I'm pretty sure Dad liked it that way.

"Really?" I asked again, giving him the option to reconsider, thereby saving me the trouble of having to choose.

"Go ahead," he said with a wry smile. It wasn't a smile of adoration necessarily, more one that illustrated he was calling my bluff. We were at a standstill in this chess match, and it was my move.

Time to buck up. Time to show him I was fearless. I took a firm hold on the rope and pushed off the bank as if kicking away on a scooter. Right at first it went well, until my feet struggled to find the security of the knot. Then they flailed in panic. My underdeveloped arm strength petered out, and, combined with the rope slime, disaster ensued. The rope slid through my hands like a slippery eel.

The water stole my breath. My bulky jacket went heavy, functioning like a sponge, and then an anchor. I slapped the surface as I located Dad, but he made no move for assistance. Instead, he walked casually along the bank, following as I floated downstream toward a set of riffles.

"You can do it," he said, waving me in.

"I can't," I said between doggie-paddles.

"You got it."

"I can't."

"Jesus, just stand up already."

And I did. I stood up, the water hardly reaching my waist. I waded to the bank, stepped on shore, and shivered. Back at the car, Dad pulled a blanket from the trunk, swaddled me, and I dropped into the front seat. He turned on the heat full-blast.

"Why didn't you help me?"

"I didn't want to get wet," he said with that same wry smile, his eyes focused on the twisty mountain road. "That water looked cold."

"What if I'd drowned?" My hands and toes burned. My fingers had curled into an arthritic pose around the blanket. Perhaps I was being a bit overdramatic, but I wanted some sympathy—a rare commodity with my father. This time proved no different.

"Drowned? Oh, come on, I wouldn't've allowed that. Imagine your mother's reaction. I would've never heard the end of it."

The following day I was left at home with my visiting grandparents. Later that evening, my father called from the hospital; I had a new baby sister.

•

I had major issues with morning bedhead. In elementary

school, Mom, always my saint, straightened my hair with a wet comb before misting it with hairspray, but by middle school my intense fear of ridicule required a shower every morning. I had to look cool, not only to avoid mockery and laughter but also because I'd discovered girls. Jersey in the early 80s meant a feathered hairstyle, parted in the middle. No exceptions.

One night, shortly before Christmas vacation, an Arctic blast blew in. The next morning, Dad pounded into my room, all sorts of pissed off.

"Get up. No shower today. The furnace busted and our pipes froze," he said, fidgeting with his tie as he left.

Severe anxiety ensued. I sat up in bed, glanced at the mirror, and prayed my hair would be passable. Not even close. Matted on one side with a hump up top, it looked like a camel had taken a shit on my head.

Missing school rarely happened. I had to be on my deathbed before Dad would allow it, and even then it was a struggle. I huddled beneath the covers, listening as he fumbled around in his room. If I could remain covert, invisible, hidden until he left, I'd persuade Mom to let me stay home. She was a bit more pliable. Sympathetic. Compassionate.

Dad's bureau drawers scraped open and closed, loose change jingling as he filled his pockets, then a faint mumbling as he talked to my mother downstairs in the kitchen. His departure was imminent. I waited for the sweet sound of the front door opening. But instead, heavy footsteps padded up the stairs and then down the hallway. My stomach sank. He hadn't forgotten.

"What the hell're you doing?" he said. "Get up. On the double. Let's go."

I poked my head from the covers, peeked in the mirror again. The unavoidable humiliation I'd suffer at school was already setting in.

"I can't go today. Please. My hair."

"Are you kidding? Get up and get ready. Double time, soldier."

"I can't go if I don't wash my hair."

The blankets flew off the bed. I went fetal.

"To the tub, right now. I'll wash your hair for Christ's sake." He left, but curiously headed toward the kitchen instead of the bathroom.

I moped down the hall, hugging myself for warmth. For comfort. I nearly cried, anticipating my peers' cruel words. From downstairs in the kitchen, pots and pans clanked. I had no idea what my father was up to.

"Okay, pull off your shirt and lean over the tub," he said when he returned. "Hurry up or I'm going to be late." He held a long-handled pot, one Mom used for boiling potatoes.

"What're you doing?" I asked, removing my shirt. "You said the pipes froze."

"They did. Now let's get this over with."

I knelt, my bare chest grazing cold porcelain. I retreated immediately, looking back at Dad as he dipped the pot into the toilet.

"You're going to wash my hair with that?"

"It's fine. Your mother keeps it so clean we could drink out of it."

"It's toilet water, Dad."

"You want your hair washed or not? I'm trying to help."

"Just let me stay home today. Please."

"No, sir, that's a negative. I go to work, you go to school. That's your job. What do you think my boss would say if I called out because my hair was messy?"

I shrugged, knowing my response wouldn't matter.

"He'd say *tough shit*, that's what. Now lean over and let's do this."

Defeated, I bowed for the guillotine. The dark eye of the drain stared back, without compassion.

"It might be a little cold," he said, his attempt at humor.

I gripped the tub-wall as the water shocked my system, a thousand tiny icepicks stabbing my skull. He squeezed shampoo into his hand and lathered my hair. He scrubbed for a minute, massaging my scalp, then the pot smacked the inside of the toilet. He poured another round. And then another.

"Once more and the soap'll be out," he said.

"That's good enough."

"No, sir, that's a negative. Once more. If you're going to do a job, do it right."

Once finished, he threw a towel at me.

"Now get dressed and get to the bus stop. If you want to brush your teeth, there's a little left in the john," he said, chuckling. He may or may not have been joking. "That wasn't so bad, now was it?"

I remained silent as he exited. It was the first of many times I felt utterly powerless against my father. Humiliated. I wanted to hurt him but couldn't. So I stood there trembling, both from cold and from shame, wiping away the trails of toilet water that trickled down my cheeks.

During junior year of high school, my father developed a new plan for how my family would bathe. He informed us there would be no more baths, as it wasted too much water. Instead, we would start taking 'conservation showers,' a term of his own creation. He explained the intricacies at a family meeting around the dinner table.

"From now on, you will get in the shower, turn on the water, and get yourself wet. Then you'll turn it off. At that point you can wash with soap and shampoo. After you've bathed, you can turn the water back on and rinse off. It's as simple as that."

"And why are we doing this?" asked my sister. She was the only one in our family who dared question Dad. I blamed it on her naïveté and youth.

"To save water. During the war, you were lucky if you got a shower once a week, and even then it was usually dirty water from a shared barrel."

"Are we at war?" asked my sister.

"You watch it, Miss Smartypants."

There was an awkward moment as Mom and I hid smirks. Then it was my turn to continue the fight. "We have a well," I said. "We don't even pay for water, so I don't get it."

"That's not the point. We all have to do our part to conserve resources. You'll get used to it in no time. If there's one thing I hate, it's waste."

My sister and I looked at Mom for answers, for sanity, for stability. Instead, she shook her head as if to say, "Just humor him. It'll pass."

But it didn't pass. Not immediately, anyway.

Conservation showers were implemented in the early fall, when it was still warm outside. But by winter, when I turned off the water per Dad's instructions, my body shivered as I bathed—in large part because he lowered the thermostat to save on oil costs. Likewise with the hot water heater.

I cursed my father every time I stepped in the shower. I couldn't comprehend how saving an extra gallon or two of water made a damn bit of difference to the world. It wasn't as if we were in a drought or on war-time rationing. If there was some sort of logical rationale at work in my father's brain, I was missing it.

Whenever Dad wasn't home, we took showers the way every other normal person took them. But when he was there, we adhered to his policy or else chanced verbal tirades and/or punishment. Countless times I awoke to his booming voice yelling at my mother or sister as they took a 'standard' shower after forgetting to turn off the water.

"Conservation shower, goddamn it. Conservation shower."

Then I'd hear the water turn off, and I knew that one of the females in my home was ruing the very existence of Dad.

If his ranting and screaming didn't work, he'd resort to Plan B. I was once in the middle of a shower when the hot water suddenly shut off, followed by Dad's familiar mantra, "Conservation shower, goddamn it." It was only after I'd gotten out that my sister informed me he'd turned on the hot water in the kitchen sink and let it run down the drain, thereby stealing my shower water. In other words, in order to enforce his ridiculous idea, he'd been willing to waste the very water he wanted to save.

Conservation showers eventually went by the wayside, just as Mom had predicted, but not without a consolidated effort of repeatedly 'forgetting.' But there was always new irrational behavior to keep us on our toes. He once punished me for two weeks of summer vacation because I forgot to brush my teeth. Part of my sentence was sweeping the street in front of our house every day with a push broom. "I'll teach you how to brush," he said. Another time, when I was ten, we'd been on vacation and hadn't gotten home until after midnight. He'd misplaced the house key, and the spare was with the neighbor. Instead of going across the street to get it—mainly, I believe, because he was embarrassed about losing the original—he busted the lock on a basement window in order to drop me through. It was solid black down there, and I begged my mother to intervene. I clutched her pant legs, refusing to let go until he physically pried me away and forced me into the dark maw. It was as scared as I'd ever been. The house had been empty for a week, and I knew for a fact that a deranged, toothless killer—wearing overalls and a flannel—awaited my approach with a hatchet or butcher knife.

But the strange thing was, I made it. I ran up the stairs, flipped on the lights, and unlocked the door. I'd faced one of my greatest fears, the dark, and won. I'd exited an icy river and returned to shore with new found confidence. I'd gone to school, my hair feathered and looking cool, and no one was the wiser. I never forgot to brush my teeth again.

Perhaps it was all just coincidence, this correlation

between cold water and my father's eccentricities (or insanity.) My grandfather had been a bomber during World War II and a career military man, so Dad had been raised in a strict and, often times, violent household—violent by today's standards anyway. Needless to say, he obtained his military blood, his toughness, his unorthodox and controlling parenting style, honestly.

Today, when I get together with family, we're able to joke about the past—my father has mellowed tremendously with age. He now claims, having perfected "selective Alzheimer's," that he doesn't recall washing my hair with toilet water. He also states that, "If it did happen—which it didn't, but if it had—I feel sure I would've used water from the tank, not the actual bowl." Likewise with the river incident: that never happened. As for conservation showers, he doesn't deny their implementation, but he's never given a satisfactory explanation as to what the hell he was thinking.

And that's okay. I've also mellowed—and perhaps grown wiser—with age, learning that some answers aren't always necessary. Now, when I change his car's oil or remove the mower blades because his back won't allow him to bend, when I scale a ladder to trim tree branches because severe gout won't let him climb, when I remind him to pop in his hearing aids after he accuses *me* of not speaking clearly, I no longer think about that stuff. Instead, I find myself thankful that the old son-of-a-bitch is still kicking around at seventy-six. Thankful he can benefit from my help, that he *needs* my help, regardless of whether he'll ever admit it or not.

MOUNTAIN MAN

Write about a disturbing event. That was the assignment I gave my freshmen undergraduates. Most responses were standard: parents divorcing, death of a beloved grandmother, abortions, anorexia, a friend's suicide. Difficult things for eighteen-year-olds, to be sure, but certainly not uncommon. However, one student really surprised me when she wrote about her boyfriend's uncle. This uncle (I'll call him Pete) had a habit of visiting animal shelters to adopt free kittens. Once home, he'd take the rescued kittens to his barn and break their legs with a hammer, then sit in the hayloft with his .22 drinking beer. By evening, the coyotes slinked in, unable to ignore the desperate mewls. Like fish in a barrel, Pete shot the coyotes, tossed them in his truck, and in the morning drove to town for the bounty—two dollars a head.

Her poignant essay brought me back, helped me recall my first vivid experience with the death of an animal, also a kitten. I was eight and walking to the bus stop one morning when my mother's screams sent me racing home. She stood next to her car—still running, thrown in Park, only halfway backed out of the garage. Beneath the rear tire and flattened to the asphalt was a kitten, part of a feral litter who'd taken refuge in a pile of old towels and rags.

My mother, hysterical, made me hunt around the garage for the surviving kittens and then place them in

56

a paper Shoprite bag. Once I had them secured, four or five in total, I folded the top and she stapled it shut. Later, she transported them to the local shelter. My father scraped up the remains of the dead one with a garden shovel when he got home from work.

The event wasn't catastrophic for me. I don't recall being overly affected, probably because I hadn't been directly involved. Or more accurately, I hadn't been at *fault*. If I'd killed the kitten, my outlook may have been much different.

•

For my tenth birthday, I received a Daisy pump-action BB gun. My father's rule: "You can shoot all the cans and targets you want, but you will not aim at birds or other animals. Killing just to kill isn't acceptable. Understood?"

I understood. And I strictly adhered to that rule... for the first week. But I, along with my friends who were equally armed, graduated from cans and bottles quickly. Birds, chipmunks, and squirrels became more attractive targets. I felt guilty every time I took a shot, but guilt has a way of easily dissolving when you don't get caught.

One evening my parents let me stay home alone while they went to dinner. I was in the backyard with my gun as twilight settled in, pretending to shoot Newark-bound airplanes out of the sky. The far edge of our yard met a weedy field full of tall grasses and briar thickets. A perfect environment for rabbits, and, as it so happened, a large one hopped into view near the back edge of the property. As it bent to nibble, I crept forward, a stalker on the prowl. At thirty yards, I took aim.

The rabbit sat broadside—nose twitching, innocently chewing, the sun setting behind it. The curved trigger married the bend of my pointer finger perfectly. I exhaled as Dad had taught me, left eye pinched, and squeezed the metal. One shot and that rabbit dropped. It didn't stagger or attempt to run, it simply folded.

I wanted to stagger, to run, to fold. I never thought I'd hit it, nor did I think my little gun was powerful enough to kill a rabbit. I looked around for my father as if he'd staged the whole thing, some sort of test of my moral fiber. I searched the windows, expecting to see him peeking from behind the curtains, shaking his head in disappointment. But of course I saw nothing.

So I made the journey across the backyard, my face flushed, still glancing around nervously every few seconds. I kept my distance, only getting close enough to confirm what I still didn't believe. The rabbit lay on its side, motionless. I didn't observe blood, though admittedly, I didn't waste much time examining the scene either. I bolted back to the house, praying my father wouldn't discover the remains when he mowed the next day.

I had a restless night's sleep, not from guilt so much as from the anxiety of getting caught. In the morning, I casually wandered to the kill zone under the guise of innocently tossing a tennis ball to myself. If the opportunity arose, I planned to slyly dispose of the evidence by hurling the carcass into the weeds. But I didn't get that chance because the bunny was gone. I searched everywhere until, perplexed and confounded, I convinced myself I'd only stunned it, and it had hopped off after regaining consciousness. I felt enormous relief, mostly for myself. I'd avoided being found out.

The possibility that overnight some larger animal may have carried off the dead rabbit for its dinner never once crossed my mind.

•

I fancied myself a mountain man. At fourteen, I planned to move to a cabin in the Maine wilderness, most likely one I'd constructed from hand-hewn logs. I'd run trap lines, live off the land, cook venison stew in a cast iron cauldron over an open flame. I'd escape the pressures of 1980s adolescence—school, sports, girls, alcohol, drugs—and embody my inner Jerimiah Johnson. I'd stitch my clothes from beaver and raccoon pelts, create a hat made from a mink or marten. I'd earn enough from my stacks of furs to buy flour, sugar, and other sundries.

Reality, of course, was far different. I lived in a middle-class neighborhood comprised of recently built two-story homes. At the end of the cul-de-sac, however, were acres of woods still untapped by bulldozers and front-end loaders. As kids, my neighbors and I spent hours in those woods—building forts from pilfered deer stands, playing hide-and-go-seek or Capture the Flag. It was where I first gained my love of the outdoors.

I also religiously read a magazine called *Fur-Fish-Game*, which taught me about steel jaw traps, wire snares, and deadfalls. In the classifieds were ads for Viktor leg-holds. I used fifteen dollars of my lawn-mowing money and ordered some. When they arrived, I ventured to the woods and set them along the creek and various trails running the meadow's edge. All of my scouting said raccoons hunted crawdads in the stream, that a few fox might roam those fields. I had no experience, no trapping license, no permission from the landowner. I just snuck into the woods and did it.

That first night, after my traps were set, I fantasized about how proud I'd be when I caught something. But inevitably, I was disappointed the next morning; my traps held nothing. This same result would repeat itself for a month. So when I awoke one Sunday and trudged through the woods on a cool November morning, just as I had so many times before, I had no real expectations.

The set in question lay on the far side of an old rock wall which a farmer had once built to divide his fields. I checked this set every day and would freshen it occasionally with apple slices or a spoonful of canned tuna. But on this morning, a large gray fox, the size of a small German shepherd, lay on its stomach, its ears perked, its black snout resting on the fallen leaves. I was immediately confused, not fully comprehending. I took a step forward and the fox sprang to its feet, the steel trap clamped over its front right paw. He yipped and screamed, the sounds horrendous: wild, frenzied, instinctive. Nothing like a dog's bark. His orange hackles stood stiff, and he hobbled as best he could, though the few feet of trap chain didn't allow for much mobility. His gaze locked on me and never strayed.

I wanted to let him go. Badly. But there was no way to do it. In order to open the trap, I'd have to step on the release prongs, and the fox simply wouldn't allow that.

He would've attacked, viciously biting and scratching.

I needed my father. He'd know what to do. He'd save me. As I stood there, alone in the woods, I wanted to cry. I wanted Daddy to bail me out. But that wasn't an option. I heard his words echoing in my head. *You got yourself into this mess, now get yourself out.*

I didn't own a nice little .22. With a rifle, it would've been so easy. No mess, no fuss. One shot and the animal would be "dispatched"—the sugar-coated trapper's term for firing a bullet into the back of a creature's skull. Instead, I carried a wooden stick, something I'd found in my father's workshop. About as long as a baseball bat, it was essentially a dowel from a coat closet.

What happened next, as I now reflect, is nearly impossible to believe. Watching it in my mind's eye still astonishes me. It was so brutal. So primal. So violent. Today, I would never be able to go through with it.

But somehow, back then, I stepped forward, my weapon at the ready. The fox went into a fury, backtracking, but there was only so much play in the chain. When I got within a few feet, I raised the stick over my head and brought it down as if splitting a log. But I missed. The fox had darted to the side. I raised the stick and struck again. This time I connected. I heard the thud against the fox's skull the same instant the reverberations travelled through my hands and arms. Like hitting a ball off the end of a bat on a bitterly cold day.

A heavy gasp exhaled from deep within his chest. He collapsed, landing on his stomach, his legs splaying out beneath him. Yet his tail stood straight up, pointing at the trees, so I pulled back and smashed his skull again, and then again. The tail gradually drooped toward the ground in slow motion. Like a thirsty flower.

He looked beautiful. Hardly any blood leaked from the head, and only a trickle seeped from his mouth. His tongue lolled over the side of his ridged black jowls. If not for that, he would've appeared asleep instead of dead.

I prodded his ribs with my stick, still wary. When he didn't stir, I opened the trap. I hadn't brought a rucksack or basket because I'd never thought that far ahead. I had never figured I'd actually catch something. I wore a quilted flannel, so I placed it on the ground and rolled him up, his body warm, his fur amazingly soft. But the fox was longer than the jacket was wide, so his fluffy tail poked out as I carried him through the meadow like a load of firewood.

I didn't live in a rural setting with a meandering dirt road twisting through bucolic mountains. Farmers weren't standing on hillsides, tilling their fields with donkey and plow. Barefooted children wearing potato sacks didn't entertain themselves by playing marbles or mumblety-peg. I lived in a residential neighborhood in northwest New Jersey. Shiny cars, manicured lawns, paved driveways. Kids climbed on jungle gyms in their backyards. Men raked the autumn leaves while their wives turned flower beds with tiny hand shovels or culled the withered remains of perennials. Yet there I was, walking up the street with the carcass of an animal I'd just bludgeoned, its warmth seeping through the rolled-up jacket. I tried to be discreet, staring straight ahead as I struggled with the dead weight burning my arms, with the puffy tail bouncing about like a feather duster.

I dropped the bundle in my garage and rushed inside for Dad, feigning excitement. Within seconds, my father, and shortly thereafter my mother, stared in wonder at the dead animal on the concrete floor. I tried to act brave and proud, the way a mountain man might do, but inside I was already hurting. I couldn't believe what I'd done, couldn't stop thinking about that fox's family. Did he have a wife, a few hungry kits waiting for Daddy to get home from the previous night's hunt?

"Well, what do you want to do with it?" said my father. He'd always been supportive of my outdoor endeavors though he had no interest himself. I'm guessing his Vietnam background had a lot to do with that. But he was no Atticus Finch, either. He was okay with me graduating from my BB gun to hunting and trapping, figured I'd learn some good life lessons—as long as I was humane. As long as the animals never suffered.

I hoped the fox hadn't suffered, and for thirty years I've tried to convince myself that he hadn't, yet those high-pitched yips and desperate yelps argue otherwise. That hard, unrelenting steel clamped shut over his leg says he most definitely did. It's difficult to tell this story, quite honestly. In fact, as I write this, I'm on my porch, my little dog at my feet while I mindlessly rub her back with my slipper. She's thirty-five pounds, same as that fox. Has an identical fluffy tail, same pointy snout, perky ears. I can't imagine taking a baseball bat and bringing it down on her head. Three times over. It makes me uneasy to even type that sentence.

So how did I manage to strike that fox, over and

over until it was dead, at such a young age?

I had no other choice. In hindsight, I wish I'd run for my father. Together, maybe we could've somehow managed to compress those release prongs. But I didn't seek his help. I'd gone through with it on my own.

"I want to stuff him," I said, answering Dad. "Get him mounted."

My mother remained speechless, staring at that dead animal and then at her beloved son, probably wondering, "Who the hell is this boy in my garage? What on earth have I raised?" She had no stomach for it, and as she started back inside, my father said, "Margaret, can you get us a couple of trash bags?"

"Are you going to throw it away?" she said, hopeful.

"No, I guess we'll wrap it up and stick it in the box freezer."

"You're not putting that filthy thing with our food."

"It'll be fine," he said. "We'll double bag it."

My mother shook her head in disgust, muttered something inaudible.

Dad was a real champ though. He located a taxidermist, dropped off the frozen bundle, and a couple months later, for $135 (which he paid), we picked it up. The fox stood on a piece of driftwood, one paw raised (the same way my little dog does when she's curious,) his ears stiff, his teeth bared, ready to attack.

That fox stayed in my room even after I went to college. I'm pretty sure my mother closed her eyes every time she vacuumed, trying to avoid him as he snarled from the corner, partially hidden behind hanging tapestries of Hendrix and Morrison. Sometime after I'd left home for good, she instructed my father to toss it in the garbage, the cycle completed.

•

Flash forward three decades. My son, Mason, and I have a tradition. To start the new year, we go hiking. So on January 1st, 2016, we met up with my friend Grizz to explore a remote area called Bottom Creek Gorge in the mountains of Virginia. It hosts the second highest waterfall in the state, pristine mountain streams, and dilapidated Civil War-era cabins hidden in dense thickets of rhododendron. Wild, rugged land. The people who built those cabins way-back-when had called the area The Roughs, an apt name if ever there was one.

At the conclusion of our hike, after several miles of walking and talking, I noticed an odd clump along the perimeter of the parking area, nestled in a copse of dormant blackberry cane. Something seemed off. Whatever I'd glimpsed, it didn't fit with the surroundings.

We ventured over to the area and, much to our dismay, discovered two dead dogs. The black-and-white one, probably sixty pounds, lay supine, its head cranked back as if attempting to scratch its snout along the ground. The other was on its side and smaller, brownish-blond. Noticeable on the smaller one, where belly met ribs, was a red circular stain, and in the center, like a perfect bullseye, a dark purplish spot the size of a nickel. Or more accurately, the size of a substantial bullet or slug. And on the throat of the larger dog, Mason noticed a tiny hole, nearly absent of blood.

"Looks like an exit wound," said Grizz. Meaning, the dog had probably been shot in the back of the head, execution style.

Our pleasant mood vanished as an eeriness settled in. I wondered if the killer was close by, still lurking the wooded perimeter. We all said various forms of, "What the fuck? Who the hell would do this? Why?" The dogs had no collars but didn't appear wild. They weren't emaciated, their coats in good condition. We all agreed they'd been shot at close range and then driven here to be dumped.

As we walked to my car, we each pondered silently over the atrocity. Over the violence. Over the stark realization that somewhere out there, most likely nearby, a man with a gun roamed. A man who was dark, dangerous, disturbed, and capable of who-knows-what. If he'd done this to dogs, what might he do if we stumbled upon him at the wrong time, happened to cross his path when he was up to no good?

Mason's demeanor instantly changed. His face grew taut. I easily read his anxiety, which pained me. His faith in humanity had been shattered. Again. Eight years before we'd been profoundly and personally affected by the mass shooting at Virginia Tech, only minutes from our home. He'd been thirteen. A few years later, one of his friends walked into the local community college with a 12 gauge and started blasting.

Mason has travelled extensively and seen a lot of the world. He's somehow maintained a naiveté about him that's endearing. He's an optimist, likes to believe in the good in people, similar to his mother. I suppose I'm more of a realist.

•

After the dog incident, we went to a local bistro where Grizz knew everybody, including the guy who led us to our table and named the specials. In his early forties, he seemed friendly and upbeat.

We ordered, tried to stay cheerful, but the gloom was palpable as the conversation kept circling back to the dogs. We each offered theories and tried to make sense of it but ultimately remained dumbfounded. I texted the pictures I'd snapped to Grizz, who planned to forward them to the authorities.

On the way home, once Grizz departed, Mason opened up. "Basically, I'm starting to believe there're a lot of bad people in this world," he said. "They do fucked up things and have no remorse."

"Sure there are bad people out there," I said, "but I think the vast majority are good. It's just that the bad ones get the attention. Or when you witness something like those dead dogs, it's so shocking that it makes you feel like mankind is evil. But in reality, what we saw today is super rare."

I tried to convince myself that those words were true. I *wanted* to believe it, but so often life had proved me wrong. Regardless, it seemed to momentarily appease Mason. When we got home, we petted our dog with more enthusiasm than usual, showed her some extra love.

A month later, Grizz informed me that the guy who'd seated us at the bistro was dead. Keeled over from a heart attack. After I told Mason, he thought for a moment before saying, "The dead dogs still bother me more."

•

My trapping career ended the same day I bludgeoned that fox. Since then, I've done my best to avoid killing animals, but it still happens. I killed a pair of copperheads on my driveway after my dogs stumbled upon them. Had to smash them with logs from the firewood pile— the only thing at my disposal—breaking their backs. It was brutal and took much longer than I'd wanted, but I had no choice. While driving, I've hit opossums and raccoons. Ran over a squirrel on my bike once. Had to put down three different dogs, never an easy task. I've killed plenty of fish, most of which I ate. I've burned yellow jacket nests with gasoline, same goes for ant hills. I've stood on ladders and zapped wasp nests that lingered behind shutters. I've killed lots of mice and rats, with snap-traps and poison.

If nothing else, that fox has given me a better appreciation for all living things. I once ran into a rattlesnake sunning itself on a hiking trail. Using a stick, I managed to scoot it off the path without incident before my dog noticed. It was a timber rattler, extremely poisonous, but it wasn't bothering anyone; it was just doing what snakes do, trying to stay warm. I've caught a few bats, using nothing more than a bath towel, and released them unharmed. If I find a stray wasp or spider in my house, I'll capture it with a jar and let it go outside. If I throw a log in the woodstove and ants emerge from the bark, frantic as the heat intensifies, I'll extend a shovel or poker—creating a bridge—to save them. Same for stinkbugs, silverfish, earwigs or any other insects that find their way into my home—I'll catch them and let them go.

I'm not opposed to fishing or hunting. If it puts food on the table or helps maintain a healthy population, I'm all for it, as long as it's done humanely. And if something poses a direct threat to me, my family, or my dog, I'll kill it without hesitation. Mosquitoes and ticks? Dead. Termites? Exterminated. But a housefly? No, I'll open a window and attempt to usher it out. Why? Because everything has a right to live. I don't know if something as small as a fly or ant or spider is capable of feeling pain, of suffering, of fearing for its life. But I know if I was a fly or an ant or a spider, I wouldn't want to be swatted or stomped. What I'm opposed to is senseless killing for no good reason. In other words, exactly what I did to that fox.

•

When composing fiction, I often create characters similar to that unknown dog killer. I try to imagine what those sorts of people are like. Hard guys, I suppose, beaten-up by life and the world. But my characters tend to have a compassionate side, something which the reader can empathize with. But this real-life dog killer, whoever he is, has no redeeming qualities. None I can envision anyway. I imagine he and Uncle Pete, the man who broke the legs of those kittens, would get along well. As much as I'd like to deny it, these sorts of men exist in the world.

According to Oxford Dictionary, *murder* is defined as "the unlawful premeditated killing of one human being by another." But I don't agree with that definition.

The victim doesn't have to be a person. Those dogs, for example, were murdered in cold blood. Also, that fox.

I suppose my defense, if I can offer one, is that I was young. That I immediately felt horrible for what I'd done. That I learned from it. That I've tried to atone.

For what it's worth, I still feel horrible about it. And I'm still learning. And atoning.

THE HOOKERMAN'S BACKYARD

Will-o'-the-wisp:
a ghostly light seen at night over bogs, swamps,
and marshes.

Will-o'-the-wisp:
a metaphor describing something sinister
and confounding.

Long Valley, New Jersey, where i grew up in the 1970s
and '80s, is barely a dot on the map. It's a quaint
town, reminiscent of a New England village. George
Washington passed through during the Revolutionary
War. Albert Einstein ate dinner at the Long Valley Inn. A
river bisects the pastoral town center, and in the summer,
as kids, we floated it on inner tubes. A giant oak stood in
front of the General Store, and at Halloween, children
threw toilet paper high into its leafless branches. Nearby
was a two-century-old Lutheran church, as well as the
stone remnants of a crumbling sawmill. Ballantine
Lumber, my first employer, sat alongside the defunct
rail bed where trains, only a few decades earlier, stopped
to deliver pallets of bricks and kegs of nails.

Long Valley is also home to the Hookerman.
Like most good ghost stories, it's grounded—to some
degree—in fact. The particulars vary. The version I grew
up with contends that a century ago, a train was traveling
through town when a brakeman saw something. Perhaps

a bear or deer. Or maybe what caught his eye was simply a zigzag of moonlight reflecting off the South Branch of the Raritan. Regardless, as he leaned out to examine the tracks, what he definitely didn't see was a dangling tree branch. The man was ejected, his arm severing at the elbow under the crushing weight of a boxcar. His body was never found. Afterward, a strange orb began to appear, floating above the rails. As the story goes, the mysterious orange light is the brakeman's lantern as he wanders the tracks, searching for his arm. A steel hook has replaced his hand, a formidable weapon if someone dares to intervene.

Whether or not a real ghost haunts the tracks is up for debate, but there's little doubt the lights are real. Scientists who've studied the phenomena have conflicting theories. Swamp gas is one possibility. Another is that a high concentration of quartz, combined with minor seismic activity, creates electrical discharges in the form of ball lightning.

When I was growing up, we sure as hell hadn't been privy to any scientific research. No, back then we took the Hookerman at face value; he was absolutely real and would kill you, period. As much as I'd like to claim otherwise, I've never witnessed the lights or seen any convincing pictures or evidence. A YouTube search produces grainy amateur videos, but the images aren't exactly compelling. But that's part of the allure, right? After all, ghosts can't be captured on film. Everybody knows that.

I played along those tracks as a boy. One of my best friends, Craig, lived nearby, and we'd often walk the rail bed, using the various dilapidated bridges and trestles to cross the river to get to the pizzeria. The rails had been removed, but cinders and rotted ties were still scattered about, the smoky, intoxicating fumes of creosote sometimes lingering on hot summer days.

One late October afternoon, as we crossed a trestle, we spotted an empty folding-chair blocking our path. Craig picked it up, about to throw it into the river (because that's what thirteen-year-old boys did, after all) when a man's voice boomed, "Put that down."

Craig froze, still holding the chair, and we both glanced around. We saw nothing. "Don't do it," said the voice, and this time I pinpointed the location. Standing in the crotch of a sycamore, thirty feet off the ground, was a bearded man dressed in fatigues and holding a compound bow. We took off, running without stopping until an enormous cornfield swallowed us, the dead stalks still standing, the crisp brown leaves wilted and drooping.

Once sure we hadn't been followed, our minds rapidly switched to the next bit of mischief. In this case, the corn. We transformed into NFL running backs, crushing and stomping would-be tacklers. Or better yet, we spread our arms, crucifix style—giant lords dominating the commoners—and knocked down stalks fifty at a time, the tough fibers ripping our skin.

As a boy, playing in the shadows of the Hookerman's backyard was the definition of autumn. A chill in the air, the faint smell of wood smoke, the possibility of a ghost lurking in the bottoms. It was glorious, innocent, mischievous. And just creepy enough to keep us on our toes.

•

Today, that abandoned railway is a fifteen-mile-long stretch of nature trail paralleling the twists and turns of the South Branch. But in the '70s, it was an eerie dirt path cutting through town before it meandered through farmland where ghosts lingered and older kids went to perpetrate nefarious things. There were plenty of turnouts where teenagers could park, hidden from the cops, to make-out with their girlfriends or have bonfire parties under the ruse of searching for the Hookerman. Going to the tracks to drink beer and smoke weed while looking for the lights was a rite of passage.

Railroads, in general, tended to create a seedy allure, and when you lived in a town that was home to a popular ghost story, the mystique was only amplified. But in 1985, something occurred near the tracks that was all too real. Something that wasn't a joke or entertaining in a ghost-story, Hookerman kind of way.

•

On Thursday, September 12, 1985, I was on the football field playing both running back and cornerback. I was a sophomore and got time on the JV and varsity squads. On that day, during a JV game, I was either tackling someone or running the ball at the same exact time a freshman, Rachel Domas, started walking home from school after missing her bus.

While I rushed for a first down, Rachel (who I didn't know, though I was acquainted with her brother, Matt, a senior) completed the first leg of her three mile journey, books and purse in tow. While a handful of parents cheered from the stands after our first score, Rachel made it to Fairview Avenue, the street she lived on. At halftime, hot and sweaty, I knelt in the end zone, sucking pulp from quartered oranges as Coach went over the game plan. Meanwhile, two miles from that football field, Rachel vanished. In the locker room, I changed out of my pads, drank Gatorade, then my father drove me home. Around the same time, Matt and his parents were in the first phases of shock, their worst fears playing out. Rachel was nowhere to be found. Her friends and family were questioned while I ate ice cream and watched television before heading to bed, oblivious that a classmate had gone missing under suspicious circumstances.

Rachel was in the Gifted and Talented program. She played the cello. Not into drugs or alcohol. As one of her friends, Shannon, recalled thirty years later, "The police grilled me on whether she could have run away, or maybe she was in '*trouble*'. I explained how in no way was that possible. Rachel was a *good* girl. Like the best, nicest, most well behaved high schooler around."

Rachel's family and friends echoed Shannon's sentiments to the lead detective, Gary Micco. Detective Micco was a rookie but had common sense. And that common sense said he absolutely believed them. Rachel walking home and not telling anyone fit perfectly with her character. But not calling to let her mother know her whereabouts, hours later, didn't.

That same evening, Detective Micco talked with employees at the Getty gas station, located on the corner a few hundred yards from her house. Those employees stated they'd seen a green Volvo parked off the road in the woods earlier that day. They mentioned this because they'd recognized the vehicle; it belonged to a former coworker. Detective Micco located the car's owner and questioned the young man for several hours. He was cooperative, said he'd had car trouble but hadn't seen Rachel. Micco's intuition told him something was off. He impounded the Volvo but was forced to release the man for lack of evidence.

At 3 a.m., twelve hours after Rachel went missing, Detective Micco and his partner, Detective George Deuchar, drove the guy home. As soon as they dropped him off, they both felt they were making a huge mistake, but without any evidence, they were stuck. At 4 a.m., the detectives explored the abandoned railroad tracks near Rachel's home. The very same tracks where the Hookerman prowled, where I played as a kid. They scanned the woods and embankments but found nothing out of the ordinary.

Unbeknownst to anyone, while Micco and Deuchar patrolled the tracks, a local woman named Nancy Weber was experiencing strong visions of a brown-haired girl and an older boy in the woods. The boy smelled strongly of gasoline. His name was Michael. She envisioned an altercation and struggle. On Friday morning she talked to Detective Micco and informed him of what she'd "seen." Micco was taken aback. It was impossible for her to have known that the nineteen-year-old kid he'd interviewed the night before was named Michael. Michael Manfredonia, to be exact. And the gasoline smell? Michael had once pumped gas at the Getty station, but again, Nancy couldn't have been privy to that information. Micco certainly found it curious but dealing with a self-proclaimed psychic wasn't at the top of his priority list. Before he got off the phone, Nancy provided one final detail. The girl was dead.

That same Friday morning, the hallways of West Morris Central were abuzz. Teachers tried to keep us focused, but Rachel was on everyone's mind. What if something bad had happened? But that didn't seem possible. Not in Long Valley. There were conjectures, rumors—teenagers being teenagers. She'd probably gotten lost. Maybe walked the tracks. Stepped in a hole. Broke her leg. That particular Friday happened to be the 13th, and the eponymous movie franchise was in its heyday. Of course kids made Jason jokes, theorizing he'd probably abducted her. Or maybe the Hookerman snatched her instead. The rumors were exciting and weird. It hadn't gotten real yet.

In the early afternoon, walking through the cluttered hallway, Rachel's brother passed. Matt was thin with light hair cut short on the sides, long in back—mullet style. Work boots, jeans, denim jacket. What struck me were his eyes: bugged and glassy. He stared straight ahead, dazed, while everyone gawked. I wondered why he was even in school. Did his parents push him? Did the police advise, "Follow your normal routine. We'll find her soon." Maybe he chose to go of his own accord. Perhaps that was preferable to his mother's wails, to his father's unraveling. I don't know. But witnessing him that day—staring blankly at a screen of horror only he could see—was unsettling.

Thirty years later, I talked with a former friend and classmate of Matt's named Mark. He told me, "I saw

Matt in the hallway that day and ignorantly said, 'I heard your sister's missing. What's going on?' Matt looked at me, didn't say a word, and started crying. I didn't know what to do, so I tried to comfort him."

I asked Mark, "Did you feel guilty after saying that?" implying that perhaps he'd been insensitive. He replied, "I don't think anyone outside the family conceivably thought anything bad had happened. But when Matt started crying, it hit home. I think he knew something horrible may have occurred."

•

I was one of two sophomores who dressed-out for varsity. Friday afternoons were our easy day. No pads, no wind sprints, no conditioning. I stood near the end zone, shagging punts while my assistant coach, Mr. McCloskey, shot the shit with me.

As we chatted, something thrummed in the distance, like the heavy bass from a passing teenager's car. It was the pulse of a low flying helicopter. The chopper appeared over the distant treetops, then buzzed the football field, flying so low I saw men with binoculars leaning out the side.

Mr. McCloskey spun a ball between his hands. He had a strange face tic, where he would blink in a sluggish, exaggerated way. Like closing his eyes in slow-motion. "They're searching for that missing girl," he said.

"Yeah," I replied, though I hadn't actually made the connection. I'd been consumed with practice. I'd forgotten about Rachel. Forgotten about Matt in the hallway. "What do you think happened, Mr. M?"

He blinked lethargically, spun the ball on his finger like a basketball, shrugged. "I don't know. But it doesn't seem good."

•

Friday evening, more helicopters. Police informed partying teenagers to stay indoors while the choppers searched with spotlights. Were they looking for Rachel? Or an assailant? Both? We didn't know. We were teenagers, immune and immortal. It was fun to speculate. Still not scary. Still not real.

Matt and his parents had endured over twenty-four hours without information. As they sat in their living room or paced the halls, every minute must have been nauseating. They'd have to survive another torturous night before they'd get any news.

On Saturday afternoon, the varsity game went on as scheduled. I mainly hugged the sidelines, only playing on Special Teams. After the game, the cheerleaders sang us the school song, them with their plaid skirts, bare legs, and poofy hair, rocking side-to-side, while we, the football players, ogled them. As the cheerleaders swayed, locked arm-in-arm, I had no thoughts of Rachel. Her name wasn't mentioned during the game or in the locker room. What none of us knew yet, as the bubbly singing continued, was that the police had made a discovery.

Around kickoff, Detective Deuchar had received a call from a search team member. They'd found Rachel's purse in the woods. And then a shoe. Deuchar hoped she had just gotten lost or disoriented, but by the time he arrived, the news had grown far more chilling.

Rachel lay dead in the woods, in the same general area as the railroad tracks. She'd been stabbed twenty-six times in the chest and back. She'd been raped. She'd been dumped in a ditch along a trail and covered with sticks, rocks, and leaves. She'd still been alive when her killer left her for dead. She'd only been fourteen.

That afternoon, Detectives Micco and Deuchar drove to the Manfredonia residence where Michael lived with his parents. They planned to arrest him but discovered he'd jumped out a bathroom window. An all-out manhunt ensued, complete with tracking dogs.

But on Saturday evening, none of that information had been released yet. More likely than not, I was getting drunk with my friends. I'm sure we discussed the missing girl, but for us, life was already moving on. There was beer to drink, girls to flirt with, fun to be had. While we tapped quarters off a table and into a shot glass, the lives of Matt and his parents had come to a standstill.

By Sunday morning, with Manfredonia still on the run and the news of Rachel's death now public, Detective Micco was desperate. That's when he thought of Nancy Weber, the psychic. He knew it was crazy, but he called her anyway. She stated she might be able to assist with Michael's whereabouts if she had a link, something he'd previously handled.

Nancy met Micco in a parking lot, and when she got into his patrol car, he handed her a metal wire from Michael's vehicle. She quickly had a vision. "He's suicidal. He's somewhere on the opposite side of the mountain from where he killed her. I see two 55 gallon oil drums nearby. He's groggy, delirious, delusional. He overdosed on something. He's on the hill watching you. He can see the police at his house."

It was true. An officer had been placed inside Michael's home with his parents' consent. Micco was overwhelmed, so he asked Nancy to make a sketch of the drums' location. She had just begun when she stopped and said, "You're going to catch him soon." Seconds later, as Micco tells it, the officer hidden inside Manfredonia's home relayed a message via walkie-talkie. "All units, he's in the house."

Micco raced to the residence. When he arrived, Michael was in an ambulance, suffering from self-inflicted razorblade wounds. Micco jumped in and read Manfredonia his rights en route to the hospital. Later it was determined Michael had been hiding in a landfill adjacent to his home, surrounded by oil drums. Tests would show he'd swallowed a large quantity of Tylenol and Sudafed. He'd told Micco he wanted to die.

Nancy's information had been hauntingly accurate.

•

I want to be clear about something. I don't believe in psychics or ghosts. The whole idea of the Hookerman is fun, sure, and I'd love to accept it as truth, but I'm a realist. And fortune tellers? Psychics? Not so much. I hadn't even heard about Nancy Weber until twenty years after Rachel's death. A television show called *Psychic Investigators* ran an episode on the murder. Detectives Micco and Deuchar were interviewed, as was Nancy. I found them to all be genuine and credible. Even still, I'm not convinced. Maybe Nancy heard a few things over a police scanner. Maybe some of the narrative was skewed during the episode to tell a more compelling psychic story. I don't know, but supernatural activity—as intriguing as it may be—isn't something I accept. The same goes for channeling Rachel's spirit or God or angels or any other mysticism.

So how do I explain Nancy's visions? Well, I can't.

•

Based on Manfredonia's later statements, Rachel walked by as he worked on his car. They knew each other informally. The year previous, she passed the Getty station on her way to the nearby middle school, and Michael would sometimes say hello. Since Rachel was already familiar with him, perhaps she was less on guard that day. According to Michael, when he saw her, he asked her out and she rebuffed him, ridiculing his looks and attire.

Furious, he grabbed a knife from his car. "I don't like being made fun of. I'll kill myself."

Rachel supposedly said, "You're acting like a little kid. I don't care what you do."

Michael recalls pushing her down. But killing her? Stabbing her twenty-six times? He claims he doesn't remember any of that.

Manfredonia's right eye was lazy; it stared outward the same as an iguana's might. He had dark hair, a mustache. He was deemed mentally retarded, with an IQ of 78. He had no previous record, save one minor charge for theft of a radar detector.

After waiving his right to a jury trial, Michael was

tried by a judge. He was found guilty of murder, felony murder, aggravated sexual assault, kidnapping, and possession of a weapon for an unlawful purpose. On August 8, 1986, he was sentenced to life in prison.

•

It would be fair to assume that our little community was rocked. But strangely, I don't remember it that way. In fact, my reaction—as well as the town's in general—has always confused me. I didn't feel scared or worried—not during the event or afterward—and I've always wondered why. Why wasn't I more affected by such a horrific crime? Sure, I was a teenager with teenager tunnel-vision, but that didn't mean I wasn't compassionate. I wasn't insensitive or cold-blooded. So why?

Teachers didn't talk with us on that Monday when we returned to school. Not a word. No guidance counselors came to our classrooms to console us. No announcement over the intercom. The principal didn't make a statement. No assembly explaining what happened, no trite promises of "moving forward together." Nothing. One of our classmates had been brutally raped, stabbed, and murdered, and instead of counseling, we were told to go on about our day, business as usual.

I contacted a former teacher, John Borowski, to see if my recollections were accurate. I must have been misremembering. "At times," he said, "it seemed like it never happened. Back in those days, we didn't have grief counselors. [The murder] was mentioned in a faculty meeting, and I was surprised it wasn't discussed informally in classes or formally by school leadership. I think the administration blew it, but I guess they believed it best for people to deal with it in their own way. I thought then, and think now, that that was a bad idea."

Next I talked with my father. He didn't recall Rachel's death at all. Which stunned me. For one thing, my sister was seven years old in 1985. In other words, he'd had a young daughter at the time, so you'd think the incident must have affected him to some degree. Instead, not a single recollection. Yet he can regurgitate the play-by-play of any sporting event I ever participated in.

So I branched out, called a few of my oldest buddies. I asked, "What do you remember about a girl being murdered in high school?" I was intentionally vague, not wanting to skew their answers. Boog, my best man, didn't remember much. Not her name, no specifics, nothing about Manfredonia. He did remember helicopters while attending a party.

I called Craig, the friend I used to play with along the Hookerman tracks. He'd been living in the epicenter of all the action in 1985. Rachel's body was discovered a half mile from his home. From his deck, he had a perfect view of her house through the trees; he lived that close. Yet he had almost no recollection. Had no idea how she was killed or who the perpetrator was. He couldn't remember her name. At first he didn't even remember the incident. "Was she walking her dog and got kidnapped or something?"

How did they recall even less than I? Were we all that self-absorbed? Clueless? Apathetic?

In January 2016, creditdonkey.com deemed Long Valley the safest town in New Jersey. In 2015, according to NeighborhoodScout.com, Long Valley was safer than 97% of all U.S. cities.

Many people I talked with echoed those statistics, commenting on how safe Long Valley had always been. How Rachel's death simply hadn't seemed imaginable. Of how it was the first and only murder to have ever happened there. Turns out, that wasn't quite true.

In the 1930s, a woman was found hanging in her barn on Zeller's Road. The husband, a farmer, stated he'd been away at the time. Apparently there was suspicion as to whether she killed herself or he murdered her. No charges were ever filed.

In the 1950s, a Dr. Pontery and his wife had a summer house in Long Valley. One night he arrived home late from work, having driven from his practice in Jersey City. He'd forgotten his key and when he tried to enter, his wife shot him. The police classified it as a case of mistaken identity; Mrs. Pontery claimed she thought he was a burglar. She wasn't charged.

In the mid-1960s, a woman named Coleman was murdered. She was pregnant. According to local law enforcement, it's still an unsolved and open case.

So there were other incidents. But Rachel's death— the rape and stabbing of a teenaged girl—was easily the most appalling. And yet, thirty years later, it seems all but forgotten.

How many times has Matt pondered, "What if she hadn't missed the bus?" It would be impossible for him not to *what if* it. I have a younger sister, so I know that's what I would do. She'd only been seven years old back then, but I asked her about the incident anyway. "I remember it happening. And what I remember most was that afterward, I was really scared to walk to the bus stop. Even now, my worst fear is that I'll be kidnapped and raped."

How was it possible I only recalled a few particulars? That my father remembered nothing? That Boog couldn't recall her name? How could Craig, who lived within a few hundred yards of the murder scene, who would've witnessed cops and search teams swarming the area, how could he have no recollection? Yet not only had my little sister remembered it, she recalled vivid feelings. Visceral reactions.

Something clicked. I needed to talk to some *women* who'd been my age. And, oh, how things changed.

I first contacted Laura, a lifelong friend. "I knew Rachel on a casual basis because of softball. When she went missing, I was absolutely terrified because I already had something troubling going on in my life. For several years, my neighbor had been trespassing on our property and exposing himself. My mom and dad weren't confrontational, so most of what this guy did was swept under the rug. When I was at the bus stop in the mornings, he'd park his car at the corner and watch me. I'm pretty sure he was naked. So I was already living in constant fear. When Rachel disappeared, I worried I might be next.

"I heard about her body being discovered on that

Saturday night when I was babysitting. My mother called to tell me, and my stomach dropped. I immediately phoned my boyfriend, and he drove over with his shotgun to stay with me.

"I'm still frightened to walk by myself near woods, and if I do, I'm on constant alert. My biggest fear is that someone is going to stop in a van, hit me over the head, and abduct me."

Laura's story was compelling, but I wondered if her experience was skewed because of what she'd endured with her neighbor, and also because she'd known Rachel personally. So I contacted Angela, an acquaintance from high school. She hadn't known Rachel, but it didn't seem to matter; her recollection was strikingly similar to Laura's. Besides specific details, she also remembered distinctly how it affected her, just as Laura and my sister had. "I was terrified after that for many years. Particularly when it came to walking in deserted areas, especially woods. I remember thinking it could've been me. I also thought it was weird how quickly everything got back to normal at school. It was the first time I realized the world goes on without you, even when you're not here anymore."

Perhaps my lack of feeling about Rachel's death (and Boog's lack, Craig's lack, my father's) had less to do with bad memory or indifference and more to do with one simple thing: being male. Maybe I hadn't been scared because I'd never felt threatened. Maybe I realized, subliminally or otherwise, that if another abduction ever occurred, it wouldn't be *me* who the psycho came after. Almost certainly the next victim would be a female.

I'm assuming any woman reading this is thinking

something like, "Duh." Or "Um, yeah," as my wife said when I shared my profound theory. A woman's everyday reality, I was coming to realize (and I admit—embarrassedly so—that I'm late to the party), is far different from my own. Or any man's for that matter. My initial assumptions—that nobody remembered much about Rachel's death, that it hadn't affected them—was turning out to be at least 50% inaccurate. I previously mentioned Shannon, a friend of Rachel's. They had lived close to one another, used to walk to the middle school together, had sometimes said hello to Manfredonia in passing. She told me, "Rachel's murder is burned indelibly into my mind. Upon hearing [of her death], I distinctly remember the absolute sadness, confusion, and fear. It changed my life forever."

I asked Shannon if she had worried for her own safety. "I wasn't afraid for my life while it was happening. I didn't sense any kind of threat, but there was definitely greater knowledge of pervasive badness. It absolutely formed my world view. I decided right then that there was no God, and that death could come at any time. Innocence lost immediately."

•

I went through the remainder of high school unaware that a significant number of my female classmates harbored fear and anxiety. And that bothers me. I feel I should've had better intuition, or at least been cognizant of it. But as aforementioned, Rachel's murder was never talked about. Not with parents, friends, teachers, coaches. In retrospect, I believe our school's administration failed us. I'm not implying they ignored us out of malice or apathy. More likely, they had no idea what to do either; they were just as confused as their students.

A year after the event, I took a criminal justice class with a teacher named Mr. O'Connell: muscular, Vietnam vet, tough and no-nonsense. Near the term's conclusion, we took a fieldtrip to the Morris County Correctional Facility. We observed what jail was like, sat through a quasi "Scared Straight" session where prisoners talked (yelled, actually) about staying out of trouble, did a walking tour.

The inmates really put on a show as we passed their cell blocks. Hooting and hollering, pounding on doors. I don't recall being scared as much as intrigued. However, I was uncomfortable and nervous for the girls because those prisoners didn't mince words. They weren't exactly on their best behavior.

Near the tour's end, we walked single file down a narrow corridor with individual cells to our left. The isolation block. Each prisoner was locked behind a solid door with one tiny window at eye-level. We could peek in as if observing a racquetball game.

Michael Manfredonia sat in one of those cells, awaiting transfer to Trenton. At least I think so. It's how I remember it. But I keep questioning myself because it seems impossible the school would've allowed that. Unconscionable. How was I permitted to observe, firsthand, the beast who'd killed my classmate? And I say "beast" because the entire tour experience had radiated a zoo-like feel. We'd stop and peer through windows, gawking at exotic creatures trapped in cages. Some paced, some gazed dejectedly, some growled and barked at us. And then there he was, the guy who'd viciously murdered Rachel. Only a few feet away. Only a few years older than me. A graduate of my high school. Slight of frame, hundred-and-fifty pounds, his lazy eye staring away from me, or perhaps directly at me. He wore a jumpsuit as he sat on his bed. He appeared tiny and harmless. And then I moved on, finishing the tour, more or less unaffected. I think.

It took three decades before I considered how inappropriate that field trip had been, especially if Manfredonia was indeed there. I believe at the time I was pretty psyched about it, but now I can only wonder how the girls in my class must've felt. Terrified? Sick? And Mr. O'Connell? He was so pleased. But I don't begrudge him. In fact, he was a great teacher. I assume he thought he'd truly done a good deed, illustrating the sorts of monsters who inhabited prison, including the one who'd murdered our classmate. But in hindsight, the whole incident sure seems pretty fucked up.

•

A few years ago, I went back to Long Valley for a visit. One afternoon I rode my bike along the repurposed nature trail, that same strip of bare land I'd always referred to as "the tracks." It was a flat and easy ride, the path composed of crushed cinders as it followed the meanderings of the South Branch.

As I rode along, I was struck by an overwhelming sense of tranquility. The route was lovely and bucolic. And yet, the presence of the Hookerman still hovered. Not in a scary way, but more in a fun and nostalgic way.

In certain spots, overhanging branches enclosed the path and created a claustrophobic, tunnel-like feel. It was easy to imagine a ghostly creature roaming with a lantern just after dark, searching for his missing arm.

But what was impossible to imagine was that a horrific murder had once taken place along that rail bed. When I approached the general area where Rachel's body had been discovered, I found no marker. No memorial. Nothing dedicated to her memory. If you were an out-of-town tourist hiking along, you'd never know something had once gone terribly wrong there. But I wasn't a tourist, and I did know. As I passed by, the incident popped into my mind for a few seconds, and then, as I continued pedaling, it was gone.

•

Michael Manfredonia will be eligible for parole on October 13, 2040. He will be seventy-four years old. Rachel Domas will always be fourteen.

THE GREAT ADVENTURE

After a full day at Great Adventure, my friends and I (Boog, Harry, Erinn, and Aimee) left the amusement park when it closed at 10pm. Aimee, the only one old enough to drive, took us to the nearby McDonald's before we made the ninety minute trek home. We were heading back to the car when I noticed several men in the adjacent Wawa parking lot, standing around, smoking. Then one of them, without provocation, started running toward us, angry and agitated.

Boog and Harry quickly jumped in the backseat, while Erinn got in front and I squeezed in next to her. I slammed the door and locked it only seconds before the guy attempted to rip it open. He then pounded on the rear passenger window. He was a typical metalhead, mid-twenties, long, poofy hair, *Anthrax* t-shirt or some variation thereof. He screamed, "Which one of you gave me the finger? Which motherfucker was it?"

"Go, Aimee! Hurry up!" I yelled, but she couldn't get the old, decrepit Volvo in reverse. It was only a two seater and Erinn's legs, scrunched atop the middle console, inadvertently blocked the stick shift from engaging. Metalhead, furious, started kicking my window with his sneaker. Hard. Like karate kicks. On the third or fourth attempt, the window shattered, covering me in a spray of safety glass. He then flung his lit cigarette through the opening, which landed on my bare arm. I grabbed it by the filter and flicked it back at his face, then scooped glass from my lap and whipped it at him, trying to keep the psycho at bay. I was in no way being heroic—I was scared shitless and the glass was simply the first thing I thought of.

The girls screamed while Boog and Harry yelled, "Drive, Aimee! Drive!" Meanwhile, I kept battling with the dude as he roared, "You don't flip me off, motherfucker."

Aimee finally managed to pull away while I still chucked glass at Metalhead, tossing out handfuls as if bailing water from a sinking boat. We were hours from home, it was chilly, the car was windowless, and I had hundreds of glass fragments in my hair, down the back of my shirt, pretty much everywhere. Frightened and not knowing what else to do, we decided to drive back to Great Adventure. The parking lot was now entirely abandoned, but we located a security guard who led us to the first aid station. No doctor or nurse on duty after closing, but I was allowed to take a shower and remove the shards from my scalp. Other than a minor cigarette burn, I was uninjured.

By the time the police arrived and took our statements, it was after midnight. We had no money for a hotel, and Aimee was too tired and shaken to drive home. The security guard, feeling sorry for us, offered up the first aid station cots for the night. Then he left us to our own devices.

Suddenly, we were all alone within the confines of the largest amusement park in the greater New York City/New Jersey area. Five teenagers. Unsupervised. We were like the Griswold family at Walley World. It was a dream come true. We'd found the fifth Golden Ticket, were locked inside the Chocolate Factory, but there was no Willy Wonka to observe us, no Oompa

Loompas keeping tabs on our behavior. By two in the morning, we were running wild: sneaking underneath the wooden framework of the iconic Rolling Thunder rollercoaster; scampering up the massive track of the Sarajevo Bobsled like little children attempting to climb a slide; weaving our way under the belly of the Space Shuttle. We had free rein.

One thing we didn't discover in our escapades, however, was the Haunted Castle. Two years earlier, in 1984, a teenager with a cigarette lighter attempted to lead his friends through the dark corridors as they searched for the exit. Instead, he accidentally ignited some highly flammable material. Though it seems impossible to imagine today, the attraction hadn't been equipped with smoke alarms or sprinklers. Eight teenagers, the same age as us, asphyxiated that day, their bodies so badly charred that firefighters, for several hours after the flames were extinguished, thought the dead teens weren't actually people but mannequins instead. Horrific monsters and not innocent kids.

But while we ran around like crazed animals, those dead kids and the Haunted Castle never crossed our minds. Our only concern was bumping into the security guard who'd been so gracious. But we never saw him again, and come morning, we left without incident.

Metalhead was never captured. And for the record, it wasn't me who flipped him off. My other friends have always maintained their innocence as well, so the general consensus was that the guy just wanted to make trouble. Most likely he'd been wasted and was simply being a punk, looking for a fight. However, if truth be told, my gut still tells me there's a good chance it was Harry. He was sneaky that way.

THE CODE THAT CAN'T BE CRACKED

1970

April 20: I was born in Atlanta, Georgia.
April 29: Schmiddy was born in New York.
May 25: Nick was born in Stamford, Connecticut.

FACT

Jimi Hendrix and Janis Joplin died that year. Hendrix asphyxiated on his vomit after consuming barbiturates and alcohol. Joplin overdosed on heroin.

1977

I moved to Long Valley. There were plenty of rough-and-tumble towns in Jersey back then, but Long Valley wasn't one of them; we didn't even have a stoplight or grocery store. The neighboring town, Hackettstown, had the amenities. Shop-Rite, Golden Skillet, K-Mart, an arcade. It was also home to the M&M/Mars plant, meaning the entire world's supply of candy bars was manufactured only ten minutes from my house. The grounds were indiscreet. No bells, no whistles, no flashing lights announcing it was the Greatest Place on Earth. The only memorable thing about it, actually, was a vast parking lot.

FACT

M&M's were invented in 1941 by Forrest Mars, inspired

by a candy that soldiers ate during the Spanish Civil War—chocolate surrounded by a hard shell to prevent melting.

1981

Schmiddy and Nick became my friends in sixth grade. "Nick" was his American name, but his real name, in Hindi, meant "King of the World." And it fit. He was confident, liked to be in charge. My school was 98% white but that never bothered him, in part because he knew Schmiddy always had his back.

Schmiddy was short and wore thick glasses but carried himself exactly the opposite of whatever stereotype that description conjures. Elite athlete, good-looking, funny, charismatic. Afraid of nothing. Girls were crazy for him. He got suspended that year for throwing POP-ITS in the hallway. Whipper-snappers, as it turns out, were not appreciated by the principal of Long Valley Middle School.

FACT

The sale of POP-ITS is allowed in every state except one: New Jersey.

1982

For Nick's twelfth birthday, his father took us to a Yankee game, and Nick let me wear his glove during batting practice. As I stood near the left-field wall, a Twins player fouled off a rocket. I stuck up my arm and BAM, that baby was in the webbing. I sprinted back to Nick, thrilled.

"Where'd you get it?"

"I caught it. Swear to God."

"Holy crap," he said, admiring it like a fine jewel, genuinely happy for me. Thirty years later he admitted he'd been extremely jealous.

I stashed the mitt beneath my seat, the ball wrapped safely inside. I couldn't wait to show my father.

During the 7th inning stretch, his dad treated us to Coney dogs at the concession stand. Upon our return, I eagerly checked on my treasure only to find the glove empty. We searched beneath the seats. And everywhere else. The ball was gone. I suspected the two men behind us might've taken it, but I was powerless. They said they'd seen nothing. They were white men, and I've always wondered if racism played a factor in the theft.

FACT
It takes a sorry bastard to steal a Yankee baseball from a twelve-year-old kid.

Months later, around a campfire, I got drunk for the first time, slugging four warm Budweisers with my buddies. Hated the taste, adored the euphoria. I felt guilty, but only because I didn't want my parents to find out. For the next twenty years, I'd chase that dragon every chance I got.

BONUS FACT
Having your Yankee baseball get stolen clearly leads to alcoholism.

1983
Coolest thing about the M&M factory: Nick's father was

high up in the company, so he often brought home large candy-filled boxes. He had an entire room dedicated to that purpose: no furniture or décor, just stacked boxes lining the walls. Schmiddy and I were sometimes guinea pigs. For example, when Summit bars were invented, we advised his dad they weren't bad, but they certainly weren't Twix.

Nick had power, a candy lord as it were. Scarface gave his men cocaine, Nick tossed us a Snickers now and again.

FACT

Popular '80s jingle, sung in a maudlin tone: *M&Ms… make friends…friends…who…share with one another.*

1984

In eighth grade, my parents took Schmiddy and me to Great Adventure. A chairlift carried patrons across the amusement park, and as we floated along, Schmiddy leaned over and spat. "Try to hit somebody," he said.

What if someone looked up? Identified us? Called security? Those types of paranoid scenarios always plagued my conscience. They never seemed to cross Schmiddy's mind.

So I spat, narrowly missing a bald man. It was terrifying. And exhilarating.

We got drunk regularly, stealing from our fathers' liquor bottles. Schmiddy had already smoked a joint. We threw our first keg party. Just a pony keg, but still, we hadn't even graduated middle school yet.

We were growing up fast, and sometimes I secretly

wanted to just be a kid. Actually, what I really wanted was to be alone. Be a hermit and read books. But I wasn't confident enough to be my own person. I was considered a leader, but inside I was a follower, engrossed in the powerful, churning tide of my peers.

Schmiddy was an exceptional lacrosse attackman: quick, dodgy, tough. I was a star athlete: fast, athletic, a natural midfielder. I was as hard-nosed as Schmiddy— on the field. After a game, however, I was passive. I didn't like fights or confrontation. Schmiddy thrived on it.

One day after practice, a fight broke out. Schmiddy was wailing on JT, a bucktoothed, wise-ass kid who wasn't quite right in the head. Schmiddy's knees pinned JT's shoulders, and he pounded the kid as me, Nick, and others circled around, cheering on the violence.

The mood changed when Schmiddy started kicking JT in the face. Rapid, like gunfire, using the tip of his hard-toed cleat. Blood flew everywhere, JT's braces ripping his gums apart as he begged Schmiddy to stop. A father grabbed Schmiddy in a reverse bear-hug, tore him away. He flailed his legs, screaming, "He pulled a knife on my sister. Fucker tried to stab her." (This allegation, by the way, was never verified.)

Schmiddy was fully enraged, his level of anger and violence like nothing I'd ever seen, but it was his coldness, his absolute lack of remorse that really unnerved me.

It wouldn't be the last time I'd witness it. Not by a longshot.

FACT

On May 11th, 1984, a month after Schmiddy and I visited

Great Adventure, the Haunted Castle attraction caught fire, trapping eight teenagers. As aforementioned, they all burned to death.

1985

Sylvester Stallone's *First Blood* was on HBO, inspiring a generation of boys to become badasses. Capture the Flag was our way of doing that. Running, stalking, hiding from the enemy. Just being kids. Out in the woods, we were innocent.

It was a perfect fall day, cobalt skies. Schmiddy and I were patrolling, searching for the enemy's flag, but our heads weren't in the game. I wanted to show him my favorite place, a meadow where I often spotted feeding deer. Though none of my friends knew it, I often ventured into the woods by myself, just to be alone and experience nature. Sometimes I'd climb an old deer stand, where I'd read a book or write stories.

"Imagine," said Schmiddy, "if there's a giant Coke machine waiting for us."

"And it's free," I said. "With crushed ice."

"And hot chicks in bikinis."

"Heather Locklear and Farrah."

"Naw, dude," he said. "Farrah's old."

"Yeah, but still."

That's when we stumbled upon the enemy. Fat Tom, dressed head to toe in fatigues. He wasn't part of our normal group, but we let him play, mainly because we needed even sides. As soon as he saw us, the poor kid didn't even bother to run. "You got me," he said. "Tie me up."

And tie him up we did, to a large oak. I wrapped

a clothesline around his formidable gut and arms, not so tight it would hurt but snug enough so he couldn't escape. Tom was genial, understanding it was all in good fun.

Until it wasn't.

Schmiddy unwrapped the waxy red paper on a pack of firecrackers. "Time to teach our prisoner a lesson."

"Yeah," I said and chuckled. I figured Schmiddy would light one, toss it at Tom's boots, then we'd let him go. Standard protocol.

But Schmiddy had other ideas. He stuffed a pair of Black Cats between Tom's gut and the rope, then pulled out matches.

Tom wriggled, tried to get free, not quite panicking yet. "What're you doing?"

I stood ten feet away, still positive Schmiddy was bluffing.

Then he struck a match.

Tom freaked, frantically jostling, twisting his head side-to-side. "No. God, please don't." Schmiddy lit one of the fuses. It sizzled and then exploded. I'm sure it hurt like hell, but I think Tom wailed more from fear than actual pain. Who could blame him? He was trapped. Being tortured. His shirt soaked with sweat, the rope cutting into his stomach, bisecting him.

I stood there. Did nothing. Schmiddy lit the second firecracker as Tom blubbered and pleaded. "Why? Stop. God, why?"

I'm not positive what happened afterward. I think Schmiddy walked away. I think I untied Tom. I'd like to believe I said I was sorry, but I'm almost certain I didn't. Tom never interacted with me again, and I imagine he still carries plenty of scars. Shit, I carry a few, and I wasn't the one who got blown up. That five minute window of inaction still badly haunts my conscience. I didn't stop Schmiddy. Worse, I did nothing to help Tom.

FACT

Empire magazine chose *First Blood* as one of The 500 Greatest Movies of All Time. My fifteen-year-old self wholeheartedly agrees. (So does my forty-six-year-old self.)

1986-1988

High school was a blur. From sophomore year until graduation, I got drunk and high nearly every weekend. *Don't go to high school, go to school high.* By junior year I smoked pot daily. Before class, lunch, lacrosse practice. By senior year I was drunk five nights a week. My grades went to hell.

Occasionally my solitary, introverted side crept up, begged me to run to the deep woods. Become a hermit. Sometimes I fantasized about going to jail just so I'd have a valid excuse to be alone, to sit by myself with nothing to do but read and write.

FACT

Children who begin drinking by thirteen have a 38% higher risk of developing alcohol dependence. The risk becomes even greater for those with a family history of alcoholism.

I was screwed.

Nick liked being in control. Whether it was collecting

money for a keg or driving somewhere, he wanted the reins. He drove a boxy Chevy Caprice, and sometimes after school we headed for New York, Schmiddy shotgun, me in back. Thirty-five minutes later, we'd pop through the Holland Tunnel. Nick loved the rush, zipping through traffic, smoking, singing to Billy Joel. *"I'm in a New York state of mind."*

As soon as we spotted a dealer, always a black guy in a sweatshirt, Nick stopped along the curb. When the guy approached, he'd ask, "You a cop?"

"No, man," said Schmiddy, "I'm no cop."

"Okay, what do you want?"

The next part we had down to a science. Nick monitored the rearview, watching traffic.

"Dime-bag," said Schmiddy.

The dealer proffered a gram of weed, and then it was my turn. "Let me see it before you pay," I said. Schmiddy handed it back to me, said, "What do you think?"

I opened the tiny baggie, gave it a sniff. "Looks good."

That was Nick's cue. He punched the accelerator, darting into traffic, running red lights as the dealer gave chase. "Hey, c'mon man," I heard through the open window as I ducked, always fearing I'd catch the bullet if one of those dealers ever started shooting.

Nick was a maestro maneuvering that Caprice. Washington Square, Seventh Avenue, Holland Tunnel, back to the Promised Land of Jersey. Singing, *"Captain Jack will get you high tonight"* while I twisted a joint and lit it.

As usual, the scam was Schmiddy's idea. Always thinking of ways to beat the system. He'd say to us,

"Cops are everywhere in the Village, so what're the dealers gonna do? Shoot us? Tell the pigs we stole their drugs? Hell, no. It's perfect."

It was scary, sure, but also damn exciting.

If we had money, we bought our weed like normal, upstanding citizens. At King's Majesty, a South Bronx Jamaican record store.

"I'm not doing it this time," said Nick. "It's your turn, Scotty."

"Fine," I said, "but you gotta go with me."

"Fuck that, it's always me. Take Schmiddy."

"Naw, it's all you," said Schmiddy, slumped in the passenger seat, smoking. "C'mon, Nick, Scotty needs your nice dark skin for protection."

"Goddamnit," said Nick.

As we walked, subway tracks loomed above us. Cigarette butts, trash rolling along like tumbleweed, broken bottles lining the streets. Abandoned storefronts, graffiti-covered I-beams. That ubiquitous New York garbage odor. People who strolled by eyed me warily; I had the only white face around.

Inside, speakers cranked Bob Marley. A line of customers queued at the rear, not one of them holding a reggae record. A dreadlocked guy stood behind the counter, and when it was our turn, I dropped a twenty on the glass. He tapped a wall mirror the size and shape of an album cover. The mirror slid open and a mysterious black hand—like Thing from The Addams Family—snatched the cash. In exchange, Thing gave me a nice bag of weed, far better than two dimes in Manhattan. Not one word was ever spoken.

Back in the car, Nick said, "Always gotta have the brown guy to protect you. Don't you?" We laughed. Nick was tall, skinny, maybe weighed 150. But his dark skin helped. At least that's what we believed. In and out, five minutes tops.

I always felt safer ripping off the corner guys in Manhattan than venturing into the South Bronx. Because that got dicey sometimes. We once showed up ten minutes after a cop had been shot. Needless to say, we didn't get weed that day.

We graduated, each receiving senior superlatives. Me: Smoothest Talker. Nick: Teacher's Nightmare. Schmiddy: Most Likely to Purely Party. That was actually a category, and he won it hands down. The yearbook picture showed him with a beer bong in his mouth. I have no idea how that got past the advisor.

1990

Nick was attending Purdue.

Schmiddy was at Radford University, a semester behind after getting suspended for pummeling a kid twice his size who stole his weed.

I was at Virginia Tech, ten minutes from Schmiddy. We often partied together when we should've been studying.

FACT

Over Christmas break, the M&M plant closed for its annual cleaning. Nick and Schmiddy worked there, power-washing the giant vats encrusted with a year's worth of chocolate. I was envious.

1991

Schmiddy and I were in North Carolina, driving to a Grateful Dead show. We were smoking weed and got lost, eventually ending up on a twisty mountain road behind a big-rig attempting to climb a 9% grade. Schmiddy got impatient, said, "Fuck it" and whipped the Toyota into the opposite lane, attempting to pass on an absolute blind curve. He floored it but the little four-cylinder hatchback labored against the steep incline.

As we puttered even with the cab, the trucker looked down like we were batshit, screaming something I couldn't hear. There was no shoulder, only a guardrail protecting vehicles from plummeting hundreds of feet into the ravine. I squeezed the dashboard, bracing for whatever might come around that blind curve, and agreed unequivocally with the frantic trucker: Schmiddy was insane.

The little car finally overcame the truck, and Schmiddy cut in just as a semi barreled down the mountain toward us, angrily blaring its horn. It had been that close. Less than five seconds. We would have been obliterated.

"You're a fucking psychopath," I yelled, freaking out.

Schmiddy laughed and lit a cigarette. "Yeah, that was pretty close, huh?"

"Jesus, man. That was nuts."

Schmiddy drew on his cigarette and exaggeratedly stuck out his bottom lip, exhaling upward. His patented move. He nodded toward the glove compartment. "Pack a bowl, would ya?"

We never did find our way to that concert.

FACT

Psychopaths are wired to seek rewards at any cost. They are impulsive, have a heightened attraction to risk-taking, are highly prone to substance abuse.

1993

My son, Mason, was born. Nick's first son, Kevin, had been born the year before. Nick would have a second son, James, in 1994. Schmiddy somehow avoided the fate of fatherhood.

At a Christmas party, I saw an old friend who'd gotten into heroin. He laid out lines on the bathroom counter, offered me one. I declined. I'm not sure why—maybe because back then there was still a stigma of *only-black-dudes-from-the-projects-use-smack*. Nick declined. Schmiddy eagerly accepted.

That night, outside in the cold, I watched over him. He stood, wobbly-legged, chin to sternum. I feared he might plunge face-first into the snow. I said, "Are you okay?"

His head bobbed, but he wore a half-smile. His mumbled response as he struggled to stand, to function, still haunts me. "Dude, this is the best feeling I've ever had in my life."

It was the beginning of the end.

FACT

"Chasing the Dragon" is a metaphor for the unattainable pursuit of replicating your first heroin high.

1994-1999

I moved to the Virginia mountains, scrapping and

scrambling to provide. I painted houses, waited tables, labored on Christmas tree farms, sold firewood, did second shift factory work. My drinking worsened.

Nick was raising his boys and getting wealthy as a financial planner. He also gambled and drank heavily.

Schmiddy lived a transient lifestyle, travelling as far south as Tampa, as far west as Phoenix, before landing back in Jersey, getting hired at Allstate as a claims adjuster. He made good money but still partied hard, including the use of heroin, though nobody knew to what extent.

FACT

Heroin addicts become experts at hiding their addiction. They lie, cheat, steal. Schmiddy was a master.

2000

I got sober. No horrific event spawned my decision— no accident, no waking in a strange bed, no arrest. I'd been drinking to excess over half my life, and I was tired. Tired of getting trashed nightly, of brutal hangovers, of falling asleep at work, of self-loathing, of my bloated body, of perpetually feeling like shit.

FACT

You can beg, plead, and threaten an addict, but until they are ready to quit, you're wasting your breath.

2011

Eleven years without a drink. My son had grown into a fine young man. Straight A's, avoided trouble, didn't party. I blamed his successes on his mother, but I suppose having a sober father didn't hurt.

Nick nearly died from a torn pancreatic duct. He lost sixty pounds and also his gallbladder. The root cause: excessive drinking. His doctor said if he didn't quit, he'd die. Despite the alcoholism, he'd raised two good kids, had always put his boys first.

Schmiddy had also dropped significant weight, down to 110 pounds. He'd lost his Allstate job a decade ago, after the heroin took full control. Got busted on his lunch break, copping in Newark. Police popped him with twenty bags.

Eventually, he lost everything—apartment, car, driver's license. Arrested dozens of times. Overdosed at least twice that I know of, wound up in various hospitals, jails, halfway houses. It's believed he robbed his cousin's apartment, taking, among other things, his dead uncle's urn so he could pawn it. It's also believed he stole a wedding ring...from Nick's wife.

I ran into Schmiddy, well into his addiction. I said, "You need to be careful. Remember Lundy." Lundy was a mutual college friend who'd been found dead in a gas station bathroom. Overdosed. His girlfriend had dumped him there. She would die a few years later, also from heroin. Schmiddy replied in a voice that had gotten rough and gravelly over the years. "Yeah, but Lundy was stupid about it."

Some of Schmiddy's family essentially wrote him off. Same with his friends. But not Nick. He bailed Schmiddy out repeatedly, let him stay at his house sometimes. Nick's sons had known Schmiddy their whole lives. He was like an uncle. Those boys looked up to him in a strange sort of way, like they respected his "hardness". Schmiddy had always been charming and persuasive, oozed charisma. His enigmatic personality lured people in, myself included. People wanted Schmiddy's acceptance even when they knew he was up to no good.

FACT
A hoarse, raspy voice is a common side effect of prolonged heroin use.

2012
Schmiddy would kick for a month here, two months there, often because he was locked up. He'd been featured on Hunterdon County's "Most Wanted" website, his mugshot there for the whole world to see. The son-of-a-bitch had been doing heroin for twenty years and still looked better than most of us. Strong jawline, brown eyes staring at the camera, hint of a smirk. As if this particular life was just a game.

Then somewhere along the line, Schmiddy got clean. Had a steady job in electrical work. Made money, paid off fines. Did so well that when his lease expired, Nick offered him a free room.

Nick had gotten divorced so he had extra space. He paid for food, cigarettes, even took Schmiddy and the boys on golf outings to Vegas and Florida.

Late that spring I stopped by. Kevin was home from college, James still in high school, Schmiddy and Nick both sober. It was like a fancy rehab bachelor pad. Swimming pool, basketball goal, Wiffle ball games. Schmiddy kept the house neat, did the dishes, fed the dog.

After dinner that night, we sat around and watched Jeopardy, Schmiddy rubbing the dog's belly. It was significant because I'd never once seen him show affection. Maybe he'd finally turned the corner. He was back to his old self again. Funny, witty, enjoyable, something I hadn't seen in years. Smart too, nailing Final Jeopardy before Nick or I could utter anything.

In a perfect world, this is where the story would end. But we don't live in a perfect world.

At some point, unbeknownst to Nick, Schmiddy relapsed. And then things got dark.

It started with Nick's older son, Kevin. Schmiddy needed a ride to Phillipsburg, a blue-collar town on the Pennsylvania border, so Kevin drove him. In an abandoned mall parking lot, Schmiddy exited. "Wait here."

Kevin was nineteen. Not a child, certainly, but still naïve and impressionable. When Schmiddy returned, he got in the backseat, told Kevin to drive. Heading home, Kevin watched in the rearview as Schmiddy wrapped a seatbelt around his arm, poured water into a Coke cap, stirred in heroin. He dropped a cigarette filter into the mixture and drew up a dose with a hypodermic.

Kevin was frightened. Mystified. Also curious. Within a week, he drove Schmiddy into the depths of Newark every day (closer, easier, cheaper) to cop bags for them both.

And it was about to get worse.

When the summer ended, Kevin made a clean break and returned to college, so Schmiddy found himself in a tight spot. No license, no car. To get his fix, he delved lower. Went younger and more vulnerable. He went after Nick's other son: seventeen-year-old James.

James was quiet, reserved, shy. An easy target. In no time, James was hooked and driving them into Newark almost daily. It got so bad that Schmiddy would sneak into James's room at 3:30 in the morning while Nick was asleep. They'd go to Newark and return before Nick woke up. James would then stumble off to school, high and sleep deprived while Nick ate breakfast, completely unawares. And all the while, Schmiddy remained under his roof, eating his food, smoking his cigarettes, pumping his youngest child full of heroin.

It was Kevin, home on break, who figured things out and told his father. Nick was devastated. He started drinking again immediately. He blamed himself. "You invite a junkie into your house, what do you expect?"

"That's bullshit," I told him. "You were trying to help your friend. You couldn't have foreseen this. Nobody could've."

Schmiddy's actions went far beyond just being a junkie. He was disturbed, fucked in the head.

By the time the shit went down, Schmiddy had already vacated and gotten his own apartment. Turns out he'd been using other kids similarly. He'd singlehandedly sucked the life out of an entire neighborhood, exposing the next generation. One morning a mother walked into her son's bedroom to find him spread-eagle on the floor, overdosed. Good old Schmiddy's handiwork right in front of her. The boy survived, implicated Schmiddy. The cops advised it was a he said/she said situation. No proof, no arrest.

A friend informed Nick that he had connections

who could "take care of" Schmiddy. This wasn't Jersey-Sopranos-TV-bullshit. He wasn't saying it to look like a tough guy. He was dead serious. Nick declined, but I'm sure he must've considered it. I know I would've; my son was the exact same age.

I texted Schmiddy. "You've reached a new low."

His reply: "Yeah, I fucked up. But those kids knew exactly what they were doing. I didn't twist any arms, let me tell you."

Classic Schmiddy. Taking no responsibility. Blaming others.

Later, I had a heart-to-heart with Kevin. He said something I'd never considered before. "Schmiddy's a sociopath. He uses people, has no remorse. Only cares about himself."

Initially, I thought it was just a college kid regurgitating his psych professor's lecture. But then I recalled those childhood incidents with JT and Tom. How he never seemed bothered by anything. His lifelong inclinations toward violence, the dozens of bar fights I'd seen him get into. Hell, we even went at it one night in his apartment after a long night of drinking. I ended up with bruised ribs after he repeatedly kicked me. So I did a little studying and determined Kevin misdiagnosed Schmiddy. My findings pointed to *psychopath* instead.

FACT

Four traits sociopaths and psychopaths share:
- Disregard for laws and social mores
- Disregard for rights of others
- Failure to feel remorse or guilt
- Tendency to display violent behavior

Sociopaths are easily agitated, volatile, and prone to emotional outbursts, including fits of rage.

Psychopaths are unable to form emotional attachments or feel empathy, although they often have charming personalities. Psychopaths are manipulative, easily gaining people's trust. They mimic emotions, despite their inability to actually feel them, and appear normal to unsuspecting people.

2013

Schmiddy went underground, but Nick, working with police, eventually got him arrested. Cops nailed him on outstanding warrants and possession. Nick was at the hearing when Schmiddy shuffled in to the courtroom, chained to a line of other prisoners. He stared Nick down, tried to intimidate him.

Nick was permitted to speak, to tell his story. After hearing what Schmiddy had done to Nick's boys, the judge was appalled. Gave Schmiddy the maximum. One year. Schmiddy was out in six months and right back at it.

FACT

U.S. overdose deaths increased 286% between 2002 and 2013. The overdose rate in New Jersey is triple the national average. According to the CDC, opioids were involved in 33,091 deaths in 2015, and opioid overdoses have quadrupled since 1999.

2015

Over Labor Day, I went to Hackettstown to visit some old friends, Bruno and Randy. Randy lived less than a mile from the M&M factory. At one point they said,

"Come on, we're going to see Schmiddy." They were drunk, so I drove. "He lives two minutes away. In a Victorian," said Bruno.

"A Victorian?"

"Yeah," said Randy, "he's doing great."

I knew they were messing with me, but I played along until the large three-story home appeared. The wraparound porch was empty. "You're telling me Schmiddy lives there?"

"Yeah, with a bunch of Mexicans and junkies," said Bruno, laughing from the backseat as he slugged a beer. Turns out it was a halfway house. "Thought we'd bum-rush the guy. Fuck with him a little."

I drove away, relieved Schmiddy hadn't been sitting outside, glad we hadn't surprised him. I would've felt like we were kicking a suffering animal. Which is stupid, I know, because I shouldn't care about Schmiddy. But I still do.

I wonder what goes through his head on that porch, smoking and staring at traffic. Does he ever think about how he once cleaned those giant chocolate vats, Nick right at his side? Does he reflect to when we were kids, stealing free candy from Nick's house when he wasn't looking? Candy that's still produced less than a mile from that Victorian porch where he sits each evening, forty-five, addicted and broken.

I'd like to think he reminisces on occasion. Maybe of lacrosse games, when I fed him the ball as he sprinted around the crease. But in reality, I doubt it.

People ask, "Why did you stay friends with him?" It's a fair question. The only answer is, "You never met Schmiddy." His charisma was intoxicating. Scores of women fell prey to his charms. Plenty of men, too. Me, certainly. Nick, definitely.

I don't imagine Schmiddy's lost much sleep over it. I want to hate him, but I don't. I want to despise him, but I don't. Instead, I feel sorry for him. I still care about him. I can't blame a blind man because he can't see. If Schmiddy is mentally ill, and truly incapable of empathy, is it reasonable for me to blame him for his actions?

Or is that just another example of me falling for his bullshit? Of still being under his spell? I've often wondered if something traumatic happened to him when he was young. Abuse maybe. His parents were solid, so I don't see it. Perhaps he was just born that way. I don't know, but something is twisted in Schmiddy's head, something I can't begin to understand.

FACT

Psychopathy is related to a physiological defect that results in the underdevelopment of the part of the brain responsible for impulse control and emotions. Conversely, *sociopathy* is more likely the product of childhood trauma and physical/emotional abuse.

JUNE 3, 2016

Back in December, I marked fifteen years of sobriety. Nick still drinks but infrequently and in moderation. His boys are clean, sober, and doing great. Schmiddy? No idea, though his cousin told me he's doing better. Said he'd be shocked if Schmiddy was still using.

I'm not a psychologist. I don't know if Schmiddy is a sociopath, psychopath, both, or neither. Or simply a junkie. Growing up, my friends and I dismissed his behavior with "That's just Schmiddy." Or later, blamed it on his addiction.

Until Kevin mentioned it, I'd never considered Schmiddy might have a serious disorder. But it sure makes sense in hindsight. Honestly, it's yet one more reason why he's so damn intriguing. So enigmatic. He's like a code that can't be cracked. Plenty of people have tried, me included, and we've all come up empty. Which, I'm guessing, is precisely the way Schmiddy wants it.

WINDOW TO THE SOUL

In the summer of 1987, Schmiddy and I were on our way home after seeing the Grateful Dead and Bob Dylan play in Philadelphia. It was midnight, and I was driving, completely sober. Schmiddy, on the other hand, was coming down from an acid trip. The two hour journey back to Jersey had been uneventful, and we were only five minutes from his house, on a wooded back road, when a woman popped out from the trees, desperately trying to flag us down. She had long stringy hair and wore a white dress, the material thin and almost translucent, like a diaphanous curtain.

I got that heart-in-my-throat feeling when I slowed, as if I already knew this would turn out badly. Soon as I stopped, she was at my open window. "Help me," she screamed. "Please. Let me in." She frantically reached for the handle of my Impala, but it was locked. She ran around the front of the car, a blurry blemish in my headlights. She was crying, her face pale and smeared with panic. It was hard to determine her age amid the chaos, but I guessed mid-twenties.

"Leave me alone, you asshole," she screamed, looking across the hood in my direction.

Suddenly, a bearded Harley man in a ripped t-shirt stood at my door with something shiny in his fist, shoving it toward my face. "Get the fuck out of here," he yelled, his voice deep and intimidating. "Get the fuck out."

I was flummoxed and scared, not at all sure what to do. The woman slipped around to the passenger door, begging, pleading, hysterical, and used the car as a buffer to keep the Harley dude at bay. She reached for Schmiddy's door handle but because Harley was still in my face, threatening me, I hit the accelerator.

It was Schmiddy, despite the LSD, who concocted our next move. He was good that way, always thinking on the fly, regardless of how high he might've been. "Stop the car," he said.

I'd only gone thirty or forty feet when I hit the brakes. Schmiddy twisted his torso out the window. "Hey, come here, motherfucker," he yelled. He motioned with a "bring it on" wiggle of his hands, taunting Harley, daring him to give chase. I'd always admired Schmiddy's fearlessness. Even on acid, he was far tougher than any other person I'd ever met, before or since. "I'm gonna kick your ass."

It was the oldest trick in the book, luring the dumb, wicked villain away from the damsel in distress. I watched in the rearview as the big Harley dude ran through the red glow of my brake lights, bolting toward Schmiddy's side. "Punch it," he yelled, and I did, then stopped again another forty feet away, baiting him. "Come here you stupid piece of shit," yelled Schmiddy. "I'm gonna fuck you up." And the guy, like some cartoonish oaf, lumbered after us once more. This time I accelerated and took off for good. We'd drawn enough fire, had given the woman sufficient time to escape.

"Jesus, you need to call the cops," I said as I drove away, the adrenaline pumping. I still imagined the nutcase somehow chasing down my car and slitting my throat. "Call as soon as I drop you off. That guy pulled a knife."

"Dude, I'm still tripping."

When I got home, I reported the incident, told the police about the girl, about Harley wielding a knife. A half hour later, an officer rang me back. It was nearly one in the morning, and my mother wasn't at all happy. At that time in my life, receiving calls from the police late at night wasn't exactly a rare occurrence. But in this instance, I'd done nothing wrong. The cops had someone in custody, needed Schmiddy and me to come to the station to identify him.

I phoned Schmiddy and he said he was okay to drive, that he'd meet me there. Once we arrived, the officer had us sit at his desk. "We're pretty sure we've got the right guy," he said. "We didn't find a knife, but we did locate a cigarette lighter along the roadside. You think it could've been that? Instead of a knife?"

"Maybe," I said, somewhat embarrassed. "I didn't get a great look. It all happened so fast."

The cop, dark-haired and mustachioed, nodded. "You guys sit tight. I'll be back in a minute." He walked off, his uniform perfectly clean and creased, his shiny shoes creaking.

Under the bright fluorescents, Schmiddy's pupils were buttons. On the nearest wall, in a cheap frame beneath thin glass, was a pressed marijuana leaf the size of my hand.

"We should take it," whispered Schmiddy, only half-joking.

"Yeah, right."

"Man, I'm bugging out. I'm tripping in a cop-shop."

There was a distinct feeling of authority oozing from the building's pores. And a sense of sterility, the same as a hospital. "You're fine," I whispered back. "Just keep being cool. Nobody'll know."

A moment later the officer came for us. "I'm going to take you into a back room. We're questioning the suspect right now. All you have to do is look through the window and tell us if it's the guy. Okay?"

I felt heat grow across my cheeks. "What if he sees us?" I asked.

"It's a one-way mirror. He'll have no idea we're even there."

I nodded, trusting the officer, but I was nervous. What if Harley somehow saw me, identified me, remembered my face?

The dark room was little more than a broom closet, cluttered with books and crates and various pieces of equipment. There was barely enough space for the three of us to stand. "Have to keep the light off," the cop whispered, "otherwise it's possible he could see in."

My heart sank a little when I peered into the questioning room. Harley sat at a table, uncuffed, leaning on the back legs of a chair, seemingly relaxed. Smoking. I couldn't fully hear what he said, but he used his hands in a dramatic, animated way. It was the guy. He had a bandanna tied around his head, something I hadn't remembered from the original confrontation, but it was definitely him. Big and burly and hairy. He could've squashed us.

"That him?" whispered the cop.

"Yeah, that's him," said Schmiddy.

"Yeah," I agreed.

"Okay, listen, what I'm—"

I've never come up with a valid explanation for what happened next. I have no way to explain it. The one-way mirror, without any warning, shattered. I don't mean it cracked or fractured or fell out of the wall. I mean it exploded into a million pieces. Right in front of us. Harley hadn't thrown anything, none of us had touched it, the interrogating cop hadn't brushed against it. Without provocation, that mirror simply disintegrated like a termite-ridden wall. Everyone stopped. Me, the cop, Schmiddy, we all froze. Harley quit talking, staring straight into the fresh rectangular void. The interrogator did the same, as shocked as the rest of us.

"What the fuck, man?" yelled Harley as he stood up, pushing back his chair. I heard him loud and clear now. He smelled a rat. Or more accurately, saw one.

Our cop finally gathered his wits and rushed us out. Back at his desk, he said, "I have no idea what just happened. But he didn't see you, I promise. The light was off, and he's all fucked up anyway. He won't even remember this in the morning. Just go home and forget about it."

Of course, that was impossible.

In the parking lot, Schmiddy's pupils still bulged behind his glasses. "Was that for real?" he said.

"Yeah, that was for real. And that cop's full of shit. That guy saw us. He looked me dead in the eye."

"I'm never doing acid again," said Schmiddy. Then we each drove home.

I never heard another word about it. No follow-up from the cops, nothing in the local paper.

Over the years, I've told the story many times, and I don't know if people believe me or not. I can certainly understand their hesitancy. I have no explanation except that weird things happen sometimes. I could do the writerly thing and try to make far-fetched connections about one-way mirrors, about shattered glass, about it being a metaphor for turning my life around. Or perhaps it was God giving me a warning. A sign. But it wasn't any of that. It was just one of those unexplainable, bizarre things.

Today, with everyone having video recorders at their fingertips, we're seeing more and more examples of the impossible. I recently watched a dash-cam video of a guy on a speeding motorcycle who smashed into the back of a moving car. The bike disintegrated on impact while the guy did a complete front flip before landing on his feet atop the car's roof, unharmed. Without video evidence, there's no way anyone would've ever believed his story. They would've accused him of being full of shit.

So what can I say? Strange things occur sometimes. I suppose a one-way mirror has a life span, the same as everything else. And it just so happens that I was standing behind that particular mirror when its time expired. I have nothing deeper to offer, nothing more profound. There was no divine intervention at play, no stars aligning, no cosmic forces. It just happened. I was seventeen, dead sober, and Schmiddy was tripping on acid in a police station. And then a mirror exploded. The end.

AS LONG AS
YOU DON'T GET CAUGHT

The snow had been falling hard all night. I'd also been drinking hard all night. Somewhere around two in the morning, the keg finally kicked, indicating it was time to go. Karen, the party's host, had invited two distinctly different sets of friends. Us, her group from high school, home from college for the holidays, and also her friends from the Jersey shore. We'd gotten along fine as we played various drinking games like Anchor Man and Quarters. But now we were excessively drunk, and there was ten inches of snow on the ground. A general, foolproof recipe for disaster. This night would not stray from the norm.

I was the designated driver, which within my circle meant it was my night to risk getting a DWI. It's pathetic and embarrassing, but back then, going to a party and not drinking wasn't a realistic consideration. Not for me, anyway. So we rotated weekends. On this night, the good news, according to my logic, was that because of the heavy snow, the cops wouldn't be out conducting sobriety checks.

As we drunkenly spilled from Karen's house, an innocent snowball fight ensued. Eventually, my friends and I headed to my car, a four-door Chevy Celebrity I'd borrowed from my father. But then things got heated. As with most drunken brawls, the actual impetus was vague and murky, though I'm pretty sure, in this instance,

I was to blame. Two guys from the other group, one named Jimmy and another unknown (but who had a cast covering his right arm) started yelling at Nick and Schmiddy. I held a tightly packed snowball, and, at point blank range, fired it full force into Jimmy's face. And then it was on, with both sides erupting into one-on-one fights across Karen's snow-covered driveway. I got sideswiped, then chicken-winged by someone who repeatedly slammed my chest into a car. I wasn't much of a fighter to begin with, and in this case, I was useless as he wrenched my arm so far behind my back that it verged on ripping from the socket. Piercing pain shot through my shoulder, and combined with all of the alcohol, I was close to passing out. But after being slammed five or six times, I managed to break free and run. But before I made it to my car, a different guy tackled me. My ankle snapped.

I dropped into the snow, the pain sharp and far more intense than what I'd just experienced with my shoulder. Then Jimmy was right there, kicking me in the face with the toe of his work boot, hauling his leg back and swinging as hard as he could. I covered my head in a boxer's pose, letting my forearms take the brunt of his blows, but I was in serious trouble, on the ground with a bum ankle, unable to fight back. Jimmy was kicking the shit out of me. Then Schmiddy showed up, all 5'7" of him, but with a fist like a steel hammer. He clocked Jimmy in the face, hitting him so hard (as I'd later learn) that his contacts flew out like champagne corks, disappearing into the snow forever. Schmiddy pulled me up by the armpits and rushed me to my car, where I cranked the ignition as the rest of my crew jumped in.

There were five of us in total, piled in haphazardly, the windshield covered in deep snow, the driveway unplowed. But we didn't exactly have time for the particulars, considering a wild mob was outside, punching and kicking the doors and trunk. I peeled out and fishtailed down the driveway, my ankle already ballooned and pulsing. It was complete chaos, everyone screaming and yelling. Then the unmistakable sound of shattering glass, something I'd become all too familiar with over the years, exploded behind me. My entire rear windshield was gone.

I kept driving, and as I looked in my mirror, instead of a wall of snow blocking my vision, I saw a wild horde still giving chase. Apparently, the kid with the cast had run up and swung as hard as he could, using the extra weight and girth to destroy my window. My buddies in the backseat were covered with broken glass and piles of snow, now pouring in unimpeded.

I made it home, stumbled inside my parents' house, and passed out. First thing in the morning, my father busted into my room. "What the hell happened to my car?"

I tried to open my eyes, but some monster was pouring sand into them. I was half-drunk and wanted to puke, both from the alcohol and the instant surge of pain. I thought I might cry. "Got in a fight," I muttered. And then, "I need to go to the hospital. My ankle's busted."

"Goddamnit, I'm sick and tired of your bullshit. When're you going to grow up?"

It was a good question but one I wasn't ready to answer. Wasn't mature enough to answer. It would take nine more years of intensified drinking before I'd finally figure it out. Arrests and brushes with the law. Fucking up. Showing no regard for those who loved me.

I hobbled downstairs, my foot and ankle three times the size they should've been, and got in our other car. As my father pulled out, I noticed that a series of trash bags had been duct taped to cover the busted window of the Celebrity. My handiwork, as it turns out, though I had no recollection of doing so.

After an ER visit and x-rays, my ankle was only severely sprained and not broken. Karen collected money from her Shore friends to pay for the window as long as I agreed not to press charges, which was fine by me. Because it was just one of those things. Another late night drunken brawl in Jersey. Plus, I was probably more culpable than anyone else anyway. Who was I to press charges?

A few nights later, now on crutches, I went to Atlantic City with Nick and another friend, Byron, to gamble. After a losing effort on the blackjack tables, the three of us were in the poorly lit parking garage of Harrah's, heading back to the car. They were a good twenty feet ahead while I hobbled behind. That's when we heard tires screeching, followed by frantic screams. "Help me. Please help me." A woman's voice. Over and over and over.

Nick and Byron took off running toward the distant pleas, while I gimped along as fast as I could. As a general rule, stories set in parking garages rarely end happily, and this one is no different. The woman, in her mid-sixties, stood behind her car, her body shaking as if riddled with poison. Her right eye was a deep, bright red, the entire white part filled with blood. No iris or pupil was discernable, giving her the unsettling look of a demon. She was unable to see, and I'm assuming all of the bones on that side of her face—her cheek, her brow, her nose—had been shattered.

She was hysterical and in tremendous shock, but with a heavy accent, possibly Greek, she explained. "I left my husband to put my purse in the trunk. Two men in a car, two blacks, they stopped and the one jumped out. He said nothing, just hit me and took my purse. I need my husband. I have to find my husband."

We reassured her, tried to make her feel safe, then Nick and Byron, each delicately holding one of her arms, walked her back into the casino. Which left me in a dark parking garage, alone, on crutches, at the exact spot where a vicious assault had just taken place. There were no video cameras back then. No cell phones to call 9-1-1. What if the assailants returned, searching for another victim? If there was one target more attractive than a little old Greek lady all alone in a parking garage, it was probably a one-legged college kid leaning on crutches.

As the scenarios built in my head, I decided I wouldn't go down without a fight. Those crutches would be my weapons. I'd have to balance on one foot, but I planned to swing for the fence if they returned. Thankfully they didn't, but I spent a long, sobering half hour by myself, my mind flooded with violent scenarios where the outcome never ended well.

A year after the incident, an Atlantic City detective called, asking various follow-up questions. But I had nothing new to offer. As far as I'm aware, the two guys were never caught, and I have no idea how that poor old woman turned out. But I have to believe her vision was permanently damaged. At the very least, she must've had reconstructive surgery, and God only knows what sort of mental trauma she endured. The violence she'd experienced put my little ankle injury in perspective. I was young and would quickly recover. She was old and would suffer permanent scars, physical and mental, for the rest of her life.

She'd done nothing wrong, an innocent victim. It didn't seem fair, but then again, nobody ever said it was supposed to be. There's a line in a song written by Bob Dylan that my friends and I sometimes quoted while growing up. "In Jersey, anything's legal as long as you don't get caught." The song was called "Tweeter and the Monkeyman" and we often sang it proudly, like an anthem, as if it had been written just for us.

I never lived or stayed in Jersey again after that winter break, except for a few days here or there. I was done. I'd had enough. It was time to escape.

ESCAPING
JERSEY

STEPS

On my last night of drinking, a Saturday, I sat by myself from eight in the evening until eight in the morning, watching SportsCenter on a continuous loop. I put down twenty-eight beers in that timeframe, ESPN's *da-da-dunt . . . da-da-dunt* pounding my head every fifteen minutes. I didn't get started until 8 p.m.—late, for me—because the night before had been a rough one. I'd gone out with coworkers to Outback or Applebee's or somewhere similar, and really painted the town. I wasn't eating, just drinking, and I puked one particular tequila shot right back up, vomiting on a coworker's pant leg. He was disgusted and left; I kept on drinking for several more hours. So I was hurting a bit the next day. When I awoke Sunday, after the twenty-eight-beer/ESPN night, my body shook and my hands trembled as I picked the bottles off the counter, the table, the floor. In that moment, I realized I couldn't let Mason, seven years old, see such carnage anymore. On Monday morning before work, when my orange juice kept spilling over the sides of the glass despite my efforts to steady it, I finally decided to seek help. That was December 4, 2000.

Six months later, I took Mason to hike a section of the Appalachian Trail that leads to the most picturesque outcrop in the entire state of Virginia. Called McAfee Knob, it overlooks the rolling hills and farmland of the Catawba Valley, as well as distant peaks and ridges folding one after the other like pond ripples. It's a popular destination for adventurous Virginia Tech students and tourists, but it's not an easy "touristy" hike. On the way up, it's a moderate four-mile climb, gaining 1,700 feet of elevation over terrain full of rocks and roots and ups and downs. It's not a backbreaker, but it's not a light stroll in the park, either.

Joining us were my two black Lab mutts, Napoleon and Boy. Napoleon, by the way, was a female, and Boy— well, yes, Boy was a male. I'd found him in the woods a few years back; Napoleon I'd had since college. She was my first dog, now on her last legs, her hips shot and riddled with dysplasia. She had no business being there, but I wanted one last jaunt with her. She'd been my trail dog back in the day, the two of us hiking countless miles of the AT in the Virginia wilderness.

I'd taken off early from work, wanting Mason to see the sunset and some of the brilliance of Appalachia. From the time he was born, I'd promised myself I'd raise him with an appreciation and love of the outdoors. I felt it was my duty as a father, but because I was always working, I rarely got him outside. Of course, drinking all the time—or, more accurately, being hungover all the time—didn't help.

But this adventure was for me, too. I was working as a sales consultant for Verizon and hated my job. Felt absolute dread every morning, the same as I had in high school when a project or presentation was due and I was ill-prepared. If I was more than two minutes late to work, I was placed on a "step." Reach Step 3, and I was in trouble, facing reprimands and possible firing. Tardiness was only one of the ways to acquire a step. Bathroom breaks were timed and monitored. Spend too long in the john, and bam: a step. If I didn't follow a particular script when talking to customers (and the script changed often): a step. I felt handcuffed most days, but it paid well, and I had a mortgage, a son to feed, a wife to get through school.

So getting out of the office was another reason I wanted to hike: to show my son there was more to life besides swiping a card to gain entry to a cold brick building, or sitting in a cubicle answering call after call, or being yelled at by customers who wouldn't dare talk to me that way if we were face to face.

But the biggest reason was that I was struggling mightily with sobriety. I hadn't relapsed yet, but I wanted to. Getting outside, I thought, might do me some good.

I packed two liters of water, matches, snacks, a little bit of everything. The hike started off fine, the dogs out ahead, my little boy at my heels, the two of us talking about college football, his passion. It was hot, mid-June, but in the depths of the forest, it was noticeably cooler. A mile in, however, Napoleon began fading. Her hips simply couldn't handle the toil. We could turn back or press on, leaving her behind, and in a moment of poor judgment, I chose the latter. We'd been together a long time, Nap and I. She was a trail dog, after all, and I was convinced she'd rest and wait for us. So I had her lie in the mayapple and Virginia creeper along the trailside, patted her head, told her to stay, and Mason, Boy, and I tromped on.

We reached the summit with an hour of sunlight remaining. Mason was thrilled by the spectacular views, the splotches of open pasture on the hillsides, and the bucolic farmhouses, appearing as tiny as Monopoly hotels down below. It was easy to discern how the Appalachian Trail wound its way along the distant ridgelines, and I explained to him the various hikes and camping adventures Nap and I had been on, including the one where we'd run into a timber rattler while en route to McAfee. What I didn't tell him was how, whether camping solo or with friends, I almost always brought a twelve-pack along. What I didn't tell him was that when I was trapped in my cubicle in downtown Roanoke, I'd sometimes stare out the window and see the outline of McAfee Knob, calling me, taunting me, almost mocking me for the way my life had ended up.

"Someday, when you're a little older, we'll hike and camp those same places, okay?"

"Okay," he said with a smile, hoping it was true. I hoped the same but wondered if I'd still be dry when that time came. Because the idea of being sober the rest of my life still wasn't a reality. On that first day in the counselor's office, the thought of never drinking alcohol again was impossible to fathom. And that's not hyperbole. It was truly impossible to digest. What about our upcoming beach trip? My friend's wedding? After a stressful workday? Weekends? Sad times? Happy times? Football games? Basketball, baseball, freaking badminton—it didn't matter. Every occasion was an excuse to drink. The counselor wanted me to enter an inpatient program immediately. I refused, saying I could do it on my own.

In 1974, when I was four, my father took me to an Atlanta Braves game. Even at that age, I worshipped Hank Aaron. My memories of the day are, predictably, muddy. I don't recall seeing #44 take the field or even the game itself. What I do remember is my father giving me a taste of his beer. Of looking up at him with pride, of knowing, even then, that sipping that beer was slightly taboo. That I'd been allowed into the inner circle. Not too long after that, I have another memory of eating pickled sausages at a dive bar in Louisiana while my father drank and shot pool with a buddy.

The first time I got drunk, I was twelve, in a field in Jersey behind my friend's house. He swiped a twelve-pack of Budweiser during his parents' Fourth of July party, and three of us split it, drinking four warm cans each. At one point, I took a burning log from our campfire and chased my friends. I did handstands. I sang. I loved it. By junior year, I was drinking four to five times a week. By college and afterward, it was nearly every day, almost always to excess. So was it honestly realistic to think I'd be able to continue with the six months of sobriety I'd already achieved? An older drinking buddy of mine, who'd gotten sober the year before, said, "Scotty, you've lost the love of your life. It's like going through a messy divorce. Your first true love, who was always there for you, is gone."

Mason and I didn't stay at the summit until full sunset, mainly because my poor dog lay in the weeds somewhere down the trail. We had descended about a mile when we bumped into Napoleon working her way up the mountain. Her hind legs trembled, and her head drooped, but her tail faithfully wagged when she saw us. It pained me, knowing she'd soldiered on, wanting to be with us. I quickly realized there was no way she'd make it back under her own power, which meant I'd have to carry her. She was eighty pounds, and I felt every one of them when I hoisted her onto my shoulders in a fireman's carry. I held on to both sets of legs, pulling them into my chest the way an old woman might tighten her shawl. Sweat poured, sliding down my face and mixing with dog hair. Lots of dog hair. Nap was a Lab/shepherd mix, and that long fur clung to my face like a glued-on beard. The hair stuck to my lips, got in my mouth and on my tongue. My hands were of no use to remove it because they were even more covered. (And yes, I get it: *hair of the dog*.) I was soaked, matted with dog fur, and then poor Nap started farting, her ass right next to my face. The pressure on her stomach, I suppose, was too much. The stink was formidable. I walked over the rocks and debris, doing my best to keep my feet on the trail, hauling eighty pounds of deadweight for as long as I could. Then I'd have to set her down to get a break, a chore in itself; I couldn't just cast her off the way you might shed an unwanted jacket. My fatigue and frustration rose quickly, yet I continued onward, step by step. Mason tromped behind, mostly quiet now.

Exactly one week after my last drink, I went to my first AA meeting. I sat in the corner, blubbering the entire hour. I studied the people sitting around the table, at first in a condescending way. As if I didn't belong there. As if they were lowlifes. Until I heard their stories. "Hello, my name's Rhonda, and I'm an alcoholic." "Hello, Rhonda." I was exactly like them. Our struggles were the same. I *was* them.

AA was there for me in that first critical month, and I couldn't have gotten sober without it. For that I'm grateful. But I only went for a month, being a bit uncomfortable with the religious aspects. Not that they were overbearing, but I took a look at the Twelve Steps and didn't fully buy into it—except for Step Nine. Step Nine says to make direct amends to those you have harmed because of drinking. That was a tough one, but the one I knew I had to confront. I apologized to my mother for the pain and worry I'd caused her. To my wife. To some other women in my past. It wasn't easy— in fact, it was frightening—but I learned that saying "I'm sorry" isn't a sign of weakness. A real man knows when to admit he's done wrong.

My father taught me that concept early on, actually; he had done his best to make a man of me. When I was eight, he taught me how to defend myself, using his Vietnam training. "If some guy ever attacks you, jumps on top of you or whatever, here's what you do. Take this," he said, showing his pointer finger, "and jam it into the outside corner of the guy's eye. I mean, drive it deep. Then," he said, curling the end of his finger and turning it into the letter J, "you make a hook. Go toward the bridge of his nose. After that, rip with all your might, and you'll pull his eyeball right out." I was horrified and also strangely pleased. I'd been let in on a little war secret, similar to when he'd shared that sip of beer with me. I pictured Dave Rollorson, the class bully, screaming in agony as I squeezed his eyeball between my thumb and finger, maybe held it up by its stringy veins and tendons like a trophy, like Perseus with Medusa's head. "Only in extreme situations, of course. But it's the best way."

A mantra of AA is "One day at a time." It's a good thing to tell yourself, and it had served me well for the past half-year. But on the side of the mountain, I wasn't in the mood for cute little sayings or inspirational quips. As Nap grunted and farted while resting awkwardly on my shoulders, I took it one step at a time instead. One step at a time down the trail, Mason in tow and getting nervous, absolutely quiet, reticent because now I was screaming intermittently, like a crazed lunatic. The forest had quickly turned dark after sunset, the trail nearly indiscernible. The thick canopy of oak, maple, and poplar had shut out the residual light. But I'd been prepared, had brought a flashlight, which I gave to Mason, who switched the beam back and forth between us so we could both watch our steps. My fear of tripping and having to launch Nap forward as I fell was very real.

I attempted to get the sprigs of hair from my mouth by drinking water, but it did no good. And then the water ran out. I was losing it. Exhausted, angry, frustrated, thirsty. I took it out on Nap, screaming at her to walk at least a little bit to save my shoulders some agony. I booted her in the butt a few times to nudge her along. She was unable to take even one wobbly step. I'd scream at her some more, then feel guilty, as if I were a baby shaker. Everything was collapsing. Dog hair, dog farts, no water, my young son in the forest, fatigued muscles, no alcohol. At least we had the flashlight... until it died. It didn't slowly dim from weak batteries; no, it just stopped.

"Mason, goddammit, shine that thing in front of me." He dropped his head in similar fashion to Nap, as if he'd done something wrong, when in actuality it was his baby-shaker father who was completely at fault. I was the asshole, not anybody else. I screamed at the trees, the primitive exhortations more like a coping mechanism than anything, but my son and two dogs didn't know that. They only heard a man cracking up. A man who was truly losing his mind, who was freaking the fuck out. My father occasionally went into tirades, getting extremely angry over seemingly minor infractions. One of his favorite sayings was "Being a parent doesn't come with a set of instructions." That's certainly true, and I have no ill will toward my father at all, I love him with all my heart and the feeling is mutual, but I wanted to follow a slightly different template than what he'd used. So far, however, I was failing miserably.

I once raided my father's liquor cabinet and poured a lethal cocktail of various liquors into a plastic Pepsi bottle, which Nick, Boog, Schmiddy, and I happily consumed. I was sixteen. The next morning, after my night of partying, Dad called me out to the back porch where he sat, drinking coffee. He didn't accuse, question, put me on the spot, raise his voice, or show disappointment. Instead, he said, "The way I see it, you took about eight dollars worth of booze from me last night. So that's what you owe. Eight bucks." I nodded, a bit dumbfounded, and went upstairs to get the cash. Neither of us ever mentioned it again. I still don't know how he knew I had pilfered his stash. The bottles weren't marked. (I'd checked beforehand.) My only thought is that a true drunk, as I learned from experience over the years, *always* knows how much alcohol he has on hand. During my peak years, one of my biggest fears was that I might *run* out before I *passed* out. And then what would I do?

It took us two hours to get to the parking lot. After opening the Subaru's hatchback, I managed to get Nap in, resting her on her side. The dome light shadowed her face, and I vaguely saw the pain in her eyes, but also regret, as if she thought she'd disappointed me. I smoothed her fur, apologized, and felt a strong urge to cry. Nap was my child, my firstborn in a way. She'd taught me responsibility, how to nurture and care for something. Failure, once again, overwhelmed me, but at least we were all off the mountain. Until I realized Boy was missing. All of my screaming and yelling and losing my shit had apparently scared him. Mason and I stood in that dark, abandoned parking lot and beckoned for twenty minutes. He didn't show, and who could blame him? I would've been wary of me, too.

"Mason, we're going home," I said. "We'll come back in the morning."

That's when Mason lost *his* shit. He'd been so strong, so stoic, not whining, crying, or complaining through the entire ordeal, but Boy was his dog. His best friend.

"We can't leave him," he said through tears. "What if we never find him again?"

I called out futilely a few more times, but Boy was having none of it. So we got in the car and left, Mason a mess in the front seat, Nap a mess in the back seat, and me a mess for all sorts of reasons in the driver's seat. With every convenience store we passed, there was nothing I wanted to do more than grab a six-pack. Pop in, hit the cooler, swipe my card, be back in the car in nothing flat. But I didn't.

The next morning, stepping onto the deck and not being greeted by Boy's happy grin was eerie. Mason quickly got upset. I phoned in sick, then we set out.

"We'll call for him once we get there. If that doesn't

work, we'll hike the trail again. But don't worry, buddy, we'll find him." I tried to sound confident, but I wasn't so sure, and if Mason's expression was any indicator, he wasn't so sure, either. But the search was over before it began. As I pulled in, lying in the tall weeds at the edge of the parking lot was Boy, his head perked, his tail thumping. Apparently he'd forgiven me. Either that or he'd already forgotten last night's tirade. That's the great thing about dogs: they don't hold grudges.

Mason squeezed that dog's neck, and Boy was in the back seat in no time. On the way home, achy and sore but indescribably relieved, I posed a series of questions. "I wonder where Boy was? What do you think he did all night? Was he right there the whole time? Did he sleep? How long would he have waited before wandering off?"

Finally, Mason said, "Daddy, there's no way we'll ever know." I immediately shut up. The kid was far wiser than I'd ever be. Mason looked back at his dog, convinced that all was right with the world.

•

Thirteen years later, while Mason is home for winter break, I suggest a hike to McAfee Knob. Mason has grown up to be a proud Appalachian, a lover of the outdoors—camping, swimming, what have you—and his favorite thing is hiking in the Virginia mountains. As we climb, we discuss the semester, some of the architecture projects he's been working on, and also that day way back when with Napoleon and Boy, both of us laughing about how crazy it all was. What we don't discuss is that I'm still sober. That I've never relapsed.

That I've done my damnedest to be the very best father I can be.

I hope he knows that. I think he knows that. Okay, he knows that.

He attends Virginia Tech. He's my best friend, and I realize how lucky I am. Essentially, every relevant memory he has of me is when I've been sober. He's never known me any other way. He never met the all-night ESPN guy. Strangely, I don't necessarily regret those days of heavy drinking, but I'm sure glad they're over. Not once, in all my years of sobriety, have I woken up and said, "Man, I wish I had a hangover today." Not once.

I understand I've beaten the odds so far, that I'm fortunate. My father still drinks. Nearly every one of my close friends from both high school and college struggles with addiction. Mostly from alcohol, but there are chronic pot smokers, too, some pill-poppers, and of course heroin addicts. My dad once said, a year into my sobriety, that he didn't think I was really an alcoholic. A friend once told me I was a pussy for quitting drinking. I watched him throw back yet another shot and thought, *I'm sorry, who's the pussy?* What takes more balls: having a drink or *not* having one? Two of my friends are dead and buried because of alcohol, both hanging themselves in closets because they couldn't get control. Mental illness, no doubt, also played a part. Both with wives, both with two children, both permanently decimating the lives of those who loved them most. So yeah, I get how fortunate I am.

Mason is a serious student, but sometimes he goes out and drinks with his buddies. He's honest with me but also discreet. I've never seen him drunk, never smelled alcohol on his breath. He chooses to do that elsewhere, away from me. I like to imagine it is out of respect, or perhaps it's that he's embarrassed. Or maybe he imbibes only occasionally because he understands the link between alcohol and heredity, and doesn't want to follow that path.

The path we're on now has deposited us at the top of McAfee Knob. It's been a brutal winter, and we crunch through some ice patches, especially near the edge of the signature overhang, the one where everyone gets a picture taken. It's a slip and fall that would guarantee death. It's happened before. But we're cautious, fully aware of that fine line, taking it one careful step at a time.

THE LOST ART

As my wife, Jocey, and I drove toward Dallas/Fort Worth International, bloody armadillo carcasses littered the roadside the same as opossums do back home. We'd been visiting our son in Arkansas and were now on Highway 69 near Atoka, Oklahoma, heading south. That's when I noticed the inconspicuous sign. I would've missed it altogether had I not already been scanning the shoulder, vying for a solid glance at one of those strangely armored animals—a genuine curiosity to a native East Coaster.

> WARNING: HITCHHIKERS MAY BE
> ESCAPING INMATES

The sign intrigued me. Clearly, it hadn't been created without precedent; there was at least one driver out there who had a hell of a story to tell. And I appreciated that it was written in the present tense. It seemed proactive, as if the Oklahoma Department of Corrections was admitting they weren't perfect. It was also an interesting commentary on human nature. The Oklahoma DOC recognized that despite most people's innate desire to assist those in need, this area wasn't the safest place to demonstrate such altruism.

So between that warning, the decimated armadillos, and the brutal 101 degree heat, there was a sense of foreboding. But it was that message, in particular, which got me to thinking.

Somewhere buried in a box of my mother's old photographs is a picture of four-year-old me circa 1974, barefoot, wearing cutoffs and a t-shirt. My hair is shaggy, bowl-cut. An iron-on decal spans my chest, depicting a fist and giant orange thumb extended in the classic hitchhiker's pose. There's no arm, no body, no face, just a humongous thumb. The shirt reads *Keep on Truckin,* or something close, the flowy, bubbly letters smooshed together like graffiti along a highway overpass.

Unbeknownst to me, that shirt offered the first hint of what the future held in store, a clue to an unavoidable, self-fulfilling prophecy.

•

Hitchhiking, in some form or another, has always existed. A farmer, with horse and hay cart, picks up villagers walking to market, a kid let's his friend hop on the back of his bike. Hitchhikers in France at one time used baguettes instead of their thumbs to catch rides. In America, the pastime seems to have evolved in earnest around the 1920s, coinciding with the mass production of the automobile. Combine that with the vast size of the United States, the lack of public transportation, the impending Depression, and the advent seems inevitable.

My first experience with a bona fide hitchhiker happened when I was eight. My father and I were driving back from the store when we inexplicably stopped for a guy on the roadside. My mother had always emphasized the ghastly atrocities hitchhikers were capable of, had ingrained in me that *hitchhiker* equaled *bad.* As delicately as she could, she explained the gruesome horrors of kidnapping, torture, and murder. So just peeking over the windowsill and glancing at a hitchhiker produced intense anxiety; picking one up was unfathomable.

When Dad pulled over and the vagabond approached, my father reached across and rolled down my window. "Where you heading?" he said to the man. And then to me, "Jump in back."

I have no idea how the guy replied, what he looked like, how long he was with us, where we dropped him off, or what he and my father discussed. All I remember is fear. What if he attacked my father and then kidnapped me? Took me to his shack in the Jersey woods and tortured me before slitting my throat with a rusty machete?

Turns out, that didn't happen. But for an eight-year-old who'd been fed countless doomsday scenarios, who'd been warned that pedophiles lurked around every corner, hid in bathroom stalls and cruised movie theaters searching for boys like me, well, that hitchhiker might as well have been the boogeyman.

Yet not long after, at twelve, I hitchhiked for the first time. Five of my buddies and I wanted to play Donkey Kong at the pizzeria four miles away. Someone suggested we hitch. I hated the idea, was sickly nervous, but said nothing.

To better our odds, we split into two packs. The other group let us set out first, which seemed a noble gesture until shortly thereafter a car zoomed past, my friends hanging out the windows, laughing and giving us the finger. We'd been duped. However, they got dropped off halfway, so when my group caught a ride and zipped by, we made sure to let them have it twofold.

The summer air whipped through the windows as we tasted true freedom for the first time. We'd discovered we didn't have to walk everywhere. Or pedal bikes. Or beg our parents for rides. We now had another means of transportation, albeit unreliable and potentially dangerous—if not deadly.

•

As I got older, I began hitching solo. And every time I did, I worried about abduction, murder, and death. What if the driver wanted to rob me? Or rape me? Or just kill me for no reason in particular? Not once in the countless times I hitched did those thoughts *not* cross my mind.

I felt there was actual skill involved in hitchhiking, even artistic elements. My method was to walk until I heard a car approaching. I'd then turn to face the vehicle and stick out my thumb while shuffling backward. I might flash a smile and soften my eyes if it was a woman, or squint, attempting to look tough, if it was a man. Certain drivers avoided eye-contact. These were the people who in no-way-under-any-circumstances would ever pick up a hitchhiker. My mother, for example. And I understood. You are letting a questionable stranger into your world. They have no car, presumably no money, and they want something from you. So why *would* anyone ever stop?

The answer is simple: people are kind, intrinsically decent. They want to help, especially when they perceive the person in question as less fortunate. It makes them feel good, basic human nature. And it's precisely that human nature the hitchhiker counts on.

Once a car stopped, the cat-and-mouse act truly began. There was a weird, unspoken mind game that occurred, the driver thinking, "Well, he must be crazy or armed if he has the guts to hitchhike," while the hitcher thought, "Why would anyone pick me up unless they have ulterior motives?" There was a feeling-out process that never fully subsided until you'd been dropped off safely.

•

In 2014, this "kindness of strangers" idea played out before the world when two Canadian professors set their hitchhiking robot on the side of the road and then observed its travels. According to their website, "hitchBOT...traveled by itself and couldn't move on its own but required friendly humans to take it from place to place."

The functioning part of hitchBOT consisted of a torso and head—imagine a Shop-Vac canister—equipped with a GPS system and a rudimentary, electronic smiling face. Its arms and legs resembled blue pool noodles, while Wellington boots and rubber yellow gloves provided a bit of style. It was a cute little thing, impossible not to smile at when you saw it.

The website explains that "During the summer of 2014, hitchBOT hitchhiked across Canada from Halifax, Nova Scotia to Victoria, British Columbia. In just 26 days it hitched a total of 19 rides and travelled over 10,000 kilometers."

Despite the above example of selflessness and philanthropy, I didn't trust anyone when I hitchhiked.

Instead, I preferred to carry a weapon, most notably my Buck knife. But if I didn't have that handy, I'd at least find a rock and cup it in my fist. I wasn't positive how that would help, but it was better than nothing.

In the late '80s, friends of a friend (a guy and a girl) picked up a hitchhiker in Virginia. At some point, the hitchhiker bound them and forced them into the trunk before driving off as they kicked, screamed, and pleaded. They were held captive for several days until they managed to escape. I don't know the specifics, except one: deep rope-burns encircled their wrists forever after, a permanent reminder of how close they'd come.

•

My biggest adventure occurred when I was sixteen. Some senior girls who'd just graduated invited me to their rental beach house in Delaware—two hundred miles away—if I could get a ride. I was only a sophomore, but when a group of good-looking, popular, eighteen-year-olds ask you to Beach Week, well, by God, you find a way.

I sat in my room, duffle bag packed, contemplating whether or not I had the balls to go for it. That's when John Cougar's "Pink Houses" came on the radio. It spoke to me. "Ain't that America" had a *feel* to it. Freedom, hitting the road to see the country. That song was the catalyst I needed, so while my mother was busy with housework, I quietly slipped out the front door. Within three minutes, my neighbor, only a few years older, happened by. And just like that, by simply extending my thumb, I was Delaware bound.

I had no map, no GPS, no iPhone. Instead, in my pocket were some crude directions one of the girls had scratched down. I was travelling on my wits, fueled by adolescent lust, testosterone, and a strong yearning for freedom.

My wanderlust was real, as much a part of my nature as a dog's instinct to bolt after a rabbit. I needed to roam. I longed for something greater. I wasn't trying to hurt my parents or cause undue worry. They were good people. They loved me. But I wanted to explore, to fall in love and swim in rivers with beautiful carefree women just as Peter Fonda and Dennis Hopper had done in *Easy Rider*. But I was sixteen, naïve, and had a heavy dose of rebellion and foolish immortality running through my veins. I wasn't mature enough yet to comprehend how worried my mother would be once she learned her son had slipped out the back, Jack, to be his own man, Stan, and used the Jersey Turnpike to get himself free.

•

After explaining the plan to my neighbor, he drove me all the way to the Turnpike. A friendly tollbooth operator told me, "It's illegal to hitch on the pike, but if you stand just outside the entrance, cops can't touch you. You'll probably catch a lift in no time."

He was right. I stood by the stacked line of cars waiting to pay their fare, my thumb only raised thirty seconds before two black men in a two-door Lincoln told me to jump in. The passenger folded his seat forward while scrunching his chest toward the dash, and I clambered in back. Immediately, I realized I was trapped. I had no viable means of escape if things got weird.

For the next hour, they never said a word, but they gave me a sandwich and dropped me off at their exit without a hitch (sorry) and even offered advice on how to proceed.

There were numerous other rides I don't recall, except for the last one. The man claimed he was a doctor. He drove a sports car, some sort of Mazda. As soon as I entered, he clicked the automatic door locks, causing jolts of apprehension. What reasonable explanation was there for locking the doors? I fingered the Buck knife's hilt, the folded blade offering some reassurance. But not nearly enough.

Doc asked basic questions: *Where you from?...Do you play sports?... Favorite subject?*...and I answered, *New Jersey...Football and lacrosse...English*...though I never divulged the deeper truth: that I'd snuck out of my parent's house, technically a runaway. But I'd never seen it as such. I wasn't running *away* from anything as much as I was running *to* something.

As we neared the condo just south of Bethany Beach, I envisioned what I'd do if Doc continued on Route 1 instead of stopping. Would I plead with him? Stick him in the ribs if he refused to pull over?

Doc eased off the road but didn't unlock my door. I was so close, only a hundred yards from my destination. As he reached into his pocket, I mimicked him, palming the knife. But my paranoia was unwarranted. Doc didn't brandish a weapon. Instead, he held cash, seven ones. "Here," he said, "I want you to have this."

"I can't take your money. You just gave me a ride."

"Take it. Please. I've got kids your age, and if they were in your situation, I'd want people to help them."

My situation? The Atlantic roared as I opened the door. I could smell and taste the salty air. A group of girls were about to deem me a total badass for hitchhiking two hundred miles to party with them. At sixteen years old, in the summer of 1986, I wouldn't have traded *my situation* for anything.

"Thanks," I said as I exited. He confirmed all I'd discovered through hitchhiking, just as the tollbooth operator had, just as the two black men had: people were good, decent, and wanted to help. Of course, it would've only taken one deranged driver with a sick sexual fantasy to alter my naïve, rosy view of the world.

•

The same weekend of my Delaware journey, another hitchhiker, just over the Jersey border in Pennsylvania, was shot in the head. At least that's how I remember it. I think I heard it on the radio or from my mother when I called from the condo to let her know I was okay. I haven't been able to verify it, but what I can confirm is that a serial killer was indeed murdering and castrating hitchhiking young men during that same time period. A few months after my adventure, on November 24, 1986, the nude body of a hitchhiker named Jack Andrews was found at a rest stop in Litchfield, Connecticut. His genitals were missing, his nipples removed, both legs severed at mid-thigh. The case is believed to be linked to several other murders of young hitchhiking men, including Wayne Rifendifer, whose naked body was found on August 19, 1981 in a wooded area of Pennsylvania. He'd been shot in the back of the head, his genitals also removed.

Ballistics reports would later confirm that the .38 caliber weapon from the Rifendifer murder was used a year later, on June 12, 1982, to kill Marty Shook, this time all the way across the country. A few days before, Marty had left his mother's home in Sparks, Nevada, planning to hitchhike to Colorado. He never made it. A fly fisherman discovered his nude body near a canyon in Utah. He'd been shot in the back of the head, genitals removed. Similar cases were reported in Wyoming and Georgia. No suspect has ever been identified, but the killer is believed to be a truck driver since the bodies were found near major highways all across the country.

As a grown man, this disturbing information stirred reflection. If the timing had been slightly different, I could've crossed paths with that killer.

The following summer, two close girlfriends of mine convinced one of their grandfathers to drive them from New Jersey all the way to Colorado to see the Grateful Dead. When the car broke down along a highway in Ohio, the girls ditched poor grandpa and jumped into a trucker's cab, determined not to miss one note of the opening set at Red Rocks. The trucker drove them straight to the venue with no problems. They were lucky. Though it wasn't unusual to see females hitchhiking in the '70s, and to a lesser degree the '80s, it was also far more dangerous.

The most infamous hitchhiking horror story involves the brutal killings of seven girls in 1972 and

1973. Known as the Santa Rosa Hitchhiker Murders, the young women ranged in age from twelve to twenty-three. Their naked bodies were found strewn along the highways of Northern California, raped and strangled. All seven had last been seen alive while hitchhiking. There are now at least eight other cases the FBI has linked to the same killer. One of the prime suspects was the notorious Ted Bundy, who'd been in the area at the time. The murders have never been solved.

•

I can't pinpoint the last time I hitchhiked, though I believe I was in my late twenties after my alternator died in the mountainous backwoods of Virginia. I can recall, however, the last time I *picked up* a hitchhiker. It was 2004, and I'd just merged on to Interstate 81 when I saw a long-haired man in shorts, hitching. He had something in his hand, and it wasn't until after I passed that I realized he held a cane—and that the man was actually a woman. Late fifties, early sixties. I pulled over, concerned for two reasons. One, it was an older woman on the side of a major highway. Two, I'd recently seen something in the news.

"Where you heading?"

"Knoxville," she said, bending to peer through my open window, no doubt taking a quick mental inventory, getting the *feel*, making sure I checked out.

"Knoxville? That's five hours away. I'm only going thirty miles."

"That'll work," she said. "Can I throw my bag in back?"

She tossed in her duffel, then sat down, securing the metal cane between her knees. We made small talk—her name was Debra, she'd been at the local VA hospital, a Navy vet. I glanced at the odd scar on her left knee, a raised, purplish thing resembling the state of California. She planned to stay the night with a friend in Knoxville, but home was still far away.

"You came all the way up from Florida?" I said. "They don't have a VA down there?"

I don't recall her exact explanation, but she had no money, no transportation, and had been forced to hitch to Salem, Virginia to get assistance. She continued chatting, nervously rubbing her scar, and I talked nostalgically of my bygone days as a hitchhiker in New Jersey. But that news report I'd seen days before nagged at me. I felt it my duty to advise her, but I didn't want to frighten her. If I suddenly started chatting about a deranged murderer killing women exactly like herself, what might she think? I decided to stay quiet until I dropped her off.

At my exit, I pulled into a Waffle House parking lot. For some reason, it seemed important that she be outside the car before I mentioned anything. "I didn't want to freak you out while we were driving," I said, "but the FBI just released warnings of a serial killer on the prowl, targeting women along major highways."

"Oh, Jeez," she said. She glanced in both directions, as if the guy might be hiding in the tall weeds. "Around here?"

"Most of the bodies were found along roads in the Southwest, but the cops believe they're linked to similar cases around the country, including some in the mid-Atlantic."

She had one hand on her cane, the other clutching her duffle. "That's scary."

"They think he's probably a long-haul guy, finding women at truck-stops. Prostitutes, hitchhikers."

"I never take rides with truckers," she said. "That's my number one rule, no truckers."

"Well, I thought I should tell you. I couldn't forgive myself if...you know, just be careful."

She thanked me and we bid farewell. In hindsight, I wish I'd asked why she avoided truckers. Considering all the other dangers, it seemed a rule not worthy of "Number One" status.

•

After hitchBOT's successes in Canada and then Europe, the following year the founders decided their little robot was ready for the mean streets of America. On July 17, 2015, hitchBOT set out from Salem, Massachusetts, bound for San Francisco. But only two weeks in, hitchBOT encountered serious trouble. The official website doesn't provide details, only stating, "... sometimes bad things happen to good robots."

Later, in an interview with CNN, creator David Harris Smith said, "hitchBOT was designed...with a personality and all the classic elements of drama, so it had a quest, and that quest was fraught with obvious dangers."

Dangers indeed. On August 1, 2015, hitchBOT was found on the side of the road in Philadelphia, dismembered and decapitated. It had only managed

300 miles in America before meeting its violent demise. Turns out, even robots aren't immune to hitchhiking's numerous perils.

•

It's been a long time since I've hitchhiked, but I still look back on it fondly. That journey to Delaware, for example, resulted in me falling in love for the first time. And not just with any girl. She'd been one of the most popular girls in the entire school. Two years older, a cheerleading captain, it was surreal, like I'd stumbled into a John Hughes film. The feelings weren't mutual, however, and when she left for college at the end of the summer, my heart was broken. But the point is, that would've never happened if I hadn't hit the open road, thumb extended.

During my hitchhiking tenure, I encountered countless people who simply wanted to help, confirming my faith in humanity and also in the kindness of strangers. Of course, the line between good and evil is eggshell thin. I could've crossed paths with that deranged mutilator of hitchhiking boys. Or someone else just as sick.

I recall once hitching near my house when a station wagon pulled over. The driver had a long ponytail, a mustache and goatee. As I leaned in to start the initial conversation, my *feel* was off. Not glaringly so, but something intangible raised my hackles. Just then, another vehicle approached, tapping its horn.

"Hey," I said to the long-haired man as I nodded toward the other car, "that's a friend of mine. Thanks anyway." I never gave the incident another thought. Until now. It was probably nothing. Then again, who knows?

When I'd advised Debra about that serial killer, one thing I hadn't known was that the investigation was part of an FBI effort called the Highway Serial Killing Initiative. Some savvy detectives discovered that over the past thirty years, 500-plus women had been found murdered along our nation's highways, the vast majority truck-stop prostitutes and hitchhikers. Ironically, what had originally caught the investigators' eyes was an inordinate amount of victims lining the roads of Oklahoma, including Highway 69, the one my wife and I were currently on.

Twenty miles before I'd passed that sign warning of escaping inmates, I'd seen a car pulled over. A man stood outside the passenger door, talking to the driver. He was shirtless, tanned, had a backpack. My first thought was *hitchhiker*. But I quickly dismissed it. Hitchhikers simply weren't something you saw anymore.

And fifty miles before that, in Eufaula, Oklahoma, I grabbed coffee at a truck stop. As I paid, I noticed a **MISSING** flyer with a photo of a woman who looked vaguely familiar. As Jocey and I walked across that steaming parking lot, I said, "Did you see that flyer? About the missing woman?"

"Yeah."

"I think Dateline did an episode on her."

"Huh," she said before taking a sip of her coffee, only half-interested. "Scary."

We hopped back in our rental car and journeyed on, eager to get home and resume our safe and normal lives, unaware that over the years numerous hitchhikers had been dumped along that very highway, tossed out as carelessly as crushed beer cans or fast food wrappers. With no more compassion than I currently offered those mangled armadillos littering the road. In fact, those women were most likely cast-off with even less.

It's all a crapshoot, I suppose. There's good out there, and there's bad. Sometimes you roll the dice, other times you pass if you're not feeling it. Thankfully, forty-six years into this game so far, and my luck has continued to hold.

HOUSE FOR SALE
BY OWNER

craigslist
CL > new river valley > housing > real estate

October 8

House for Sale by Owner—3br, 1½ bath, charming ranch circa 1948, bathrooms renovated 2011, including ripping out rotten boards damaged by termites. No worries, exterminator used Ultra Package. Drilled through concrete + flagstone, injected powerful chemicals around home's perimeter. No termites for next 99 years—guaranteed. Okay, so there's that. And roof leaks in a few spots, though a gulley-washer needed for that to happen. There's the hole in LR which I still haven't patched where a rat chewed through the wall while wife watched Survivor on couch. (3/4 inch plywood—serious walls + indication of construction quality. They don't make 'em like this anymore.) Turns out, besides rats sneaking up from their digs in the basement (partially finished, propane fireplace, bar w/ Formica countertop,) a family of them lived in the refrigerator. No, not *in* refrigerator proper (that's disgusting) but in back next to motor + insulation. After inspection of rear of fridge, found piles of moldy dog kibble as well as acorns. Not to mention feces. Lord God, the feces. (FYI, new refrigerator installed September 2013. Sweet one too. French doors,

KitchenAid, stainless steel, no rats!) Massive Victor traps + serious poison (think bright blue Lego blocks scattered about) took care of rat problem. No more Norwegian rats in this stylish home, no sireee Bob. Wiped out those bastards, including big son-of-a-bitch (two footer, nose to tail) found on basement floor while tending the woodstove one morning. (Hell, while I'm at it, basement floods sometimes, yet here's the cool thing: water goes away on its own. No idea why/how but it's one of those, "If it ain't broke don't fix it" situations.) Anyway, used box from wife's Diet Coke twelve-pack to scoop up dead, poison-filled rat. Except, and here's the real doozy, rat wasn't actually dead. Started writhing + wriggling in my hands. Felt movements through paperboard. Freaked me the fuck out, I'll tell you, so rat was popped straight into hot woodstove and iron door slammed tight. (PapaBear woodstove included, alternate heat/cooking source during ice storms + power outages.) High-pitched screeching didn't last long, honestly, though a bit disconcerting. And before you animal rights/PETA people start judging, it was a rat, okay? In the house, okay? Squirming like an eel, w/ only a thin piece of cardboard separating my human flesh from its teeth which, do I need to remind you?, had gnawed through 3/4" plywood? Like goddamned beavers, those rats. Poison was killing him slowly anyway, so fire only expedited inevitable. No more vermin, no termites, no pests. Major purchase point if you ask me. Give a call + let's talk.

CL > new river valley > housing > real estate

October 19

House for Sale by Owner —3br, 1½ bath, unique ranch-style home. Central air/heat pump installed 2013. Quiet, middleclass neighborhood. Well, usually it's quiet. There was the incident at the little old lady's house up the road. In her mid-eighties, lived alone except for two female caregivers. First disturbance came when my son was at park next door (renovated 2012, jungle gym w/slides galore, bball court, major perk if you have children.) He witnessed a distressed boyfriend storm from house, yelling at caregiver. "You're going to hell, Tara" or something similar. Around same timeframe, I noticed occasional odd smell when sitting on deck (rebuilt + stained 2009) drinking coffee. Didn't think much of it. There's a detail shop close by, so figured just odor from chemicals slapped on some hotrod. Boy, was I wrong. One day I'm pulling out of driveway (on blind curve btw, so use caution) and see cop cars swarming old lady's place. Turns out, the two caregivers had built meth lab in basement. You heard right, a meth lab. WTF? you say. Yeah, no kidding. Yellow police tape surrounded the place for weeks. But here's the good news. Caregivers thrown in jail. Little old lady placed in retirement home, apparently none the wiser thank God. New (seemingly respectable) couple has moved in. Seriously, don't let this deter you. Charming neighborhood. Drop me a line. Great price, great house.

CL > new river valley > housing > real estate

November 4

House for Sale by Owner (price reduced)—3br, 1½ bath, renovated kitchen August 2013, fenced-in backyard, perfect for pets, safe neighborhood. Well, pretty safe. Things do happen occasionally, right? Even the best orchard has a few bad apples. One such apple lived in duplex next door. Notice past tense please: *lived* not *lives*. So it's all good now. (Full disclosure: duplex is for those on public assistance. Woman + two sons in one half of duplex are super nice. Practically raised those boys. Taught them how to shoot free throws, gave scrap wood for forts, things like that. Even secretly bought a used Wii, packed it in a box, had my son sneak over on a snowy Christmas Eve, place on front porch. Like *It's a Wonderful Life* or something. Well, maybe not the best example—damn dark movie for a Christmas flick. Anyway, next day younger boy came over, thrilled, wanting to borrow our games. Said maybe there really is a Santa Claus. I shared quick glance w/ my son. Immensely satisfying, one of many reasons such a great neighborhood.) Sorry for digression, back to the bad apple. Other half of duplex has seen fair share of transients/undesirables. Bit of a revolving door, you might say. No real problems, though, until the day I came home to find (surprise, surprise) cops up/down street, along w/ WDBJ7 news van. Cops tried serving warrant on the guy—thirty-something, living w/mama—guy opened door, started blasting, hitting cop before being shot himself. Luckily no one killed/seriously injured. Also luckily, no stray bullets hit my windows (new storm windows 2006—high-end, double paned, Energy Star approved.) Here's more good news: the dude's in prison for the next forty years, so no worries about him returning to scene of crime. Nice new family living there now. Single mother w/ two little girls + simply adorable eighty pound pit bull. Things are looking up. Send email, let's make a deal.

CL > new river valley > housing > real estate

November 15

House for Sale by Owner (dramatically reduced)—3br, 1½ bath, short drive to Virginia Tech, ¾ acre lot w/ trees + privacy, neighbors who keep to themselves. Most do anyway. There is Norma. Personally not my cup of tea, but if you like tattered American flags in the front yard, along with assorted bird baths, concrete lawn ornaments, fluorescent bug zappers, and some sort of plastic amphibian in the bushes that has a nighttime motion sensor and therefore sings "Jerimiah Was A Bullfrog" every ten minutes in the summer while you have your windows open, then Norma might just be the perfect neighbor for you. Remember being a kid and there was that house w/ the old couple who'd go apeshit if you walked on their grass? Or, God forbid, your Wiffle ball went over their fence after your friend Byron had some epiphany and suddenly fancied himself a switch-hitter and started batting lefty? That's Norma. Mid-seventies, two times a widow. She knocked on my door one day, demanding $75. When I asked why, she said $40 was for scratches on her truck bumper, which, according to her, my escaped dog (Kafka, Black Lab, God rest his soul) caused after chewing on it. After I mentioned that Kafka had never once chewed on any of *my* bumpers, not once not ever, she said it happened b/c Kafka was trying to get her cat hiding beneath the truck.

"How exactly does chewing on a bumper aid in catching a cat?" I inquired. W/O reply she handed over an estimate sheet from a local body shop. After a quick perusal, I asked, "You said $75. What's the other $35 for?"

"For my dead azaleas," she said. "When your dog wanders over, he always pees on them."

"We're in the worst drought in forty years, Norma. You think my dog killed your bushes?"

"Yes."

Which leads to yet another bonus of house. Location, location, location. Certain amenities come w/ working at/living near a college. Example: I called the university's horticulture extension agent, explained Norma's claims about Kafka's volatile piss. He stated if Kafka urinated five gallons on Norma's bushes every day for a year that might kill them, however b/c of ongoing drought any urine Kafka produced only *helped* the azaleas, not hurt them. So I gave Norma forty bucks for the bumper to wipe my hands clean of the crazy woman. A "good fences makes good neighbors" approach, yet over the years I've cleaned out her gutters/shoveled her driveway w/o being asked. She's alone, her adult son committed suicide, and what can I say, I'm a softie. Maybe you'll look in on her every once in a while, won't you, just to make sure she's okay? At any rate, give me a call. Don't know what the hell people are waiting on.

CL > new river valley > housing > real estate

November 19

House for Sale by Owner (priced to sell)—3br, 1½ bath, cozy family home, landscaping overhaul 2012, driveway resurfaced 2009, large windows offer abundant sunshine/panoramic views, especially from massive LR picture window (all windows replaced 2006, bullet-hole free, see previous post.) Windows are wonderful way to see goings on of neighborhood. Example: two days ago I'm sitting on couch when I hear distraught screams. "You fucking asshole. I hate you. I fucking hate you." I decided that was worth getting up for. Cattycorner is Travis's house. Twenty-ish young man, bearded, overweight, something of a wannabe Harley dude. Known him since he was a kid when he'd come over to play w/ my son in rat infested basement (see previous post, no longer infested.) Always felt sorry for him b/c his mother was never around +/or when she was around always had a different boyfriend. Regardless, Travis now lived alone. On this particular morning it wasn't Travis but some other twenty-something doing the yelling, standing in driveway, ranting, and I watched (somewhat amused I must admit) as he paced by Travis's car: beat-up old thing of some make/model I'm not familiar w/. Distressed guy raised his arm, hand grasping something, and came down full force on the windshield. Three times. Smash, smash, smash. Then tossed whatever it was, hammer maybe? into adjoining neighbor's yard +

walked quickly down the road. I ran from small window to picture window to continue observations. Only then did Travis come out, talking on his cell. You'd figure cops, right? Wrong. Cops never showed. Don't know if it was romance gone south (never pegged Travis as gay, but who knows?) or maybe a bad drug deal, but whatever, he sure didn't call the police. Regardless, point is this: now-deeply-discounted-home offers 360 degree views. Buyer's market, motivated seller. Great investment opportunity. Wait too long, this baby'll be gonzo.

CL > new river valley > housing > real estate

December 9

House for Sale by Owner (absolute rock-bottom price)—3br, 1½ bath. Revived downtown only three minute walk. Farmer's market on Thursdays. Spacious, comfortable home in thriving neighborhood on rebound. Speaking of which, you + your children need not worry about neighbor, Michael, who last Wednesday was arrested. I'd just gotten home when Norma yelled for me (yes, truck bumper lady—please see earlier post.) "Scott, come here," she said, beckoning from her doorway. This was odd, this never happened, Norma and I didn't talk. After I crossed the street, she half-whispered, "What happened at Michael's today?" I had no idea what she was talking about, but I must back up for a second. Michael's a bit of an odd duck. Mid-forties, skinny, balding, walks slightly hunched. Might say scarecrow-ish. Works as bagger at grocery store

(Kroger, btw, only a half mile away. Bonus.)

Norma continued, "Police cars were all over the place this morning. Cops dressed in full armor, guns drawn, two of them holding a battering ram."

"A battering ram?"

"Yes. You think it's drugs?"

"Norma, I have no idea."

"You know, he was arrested a few months back."

"Arrested?" I said. "Michael?" Clearly I hadn't been paying as much attention to the neighborhood as I'd thought. "For what?"

"Sex with children."

"What? In our nice little neighborhood?" I said, blown away though I had to take pause and consider the source. After all, this was the woman who accused my dog of assaulting her bumper. The woman who once sold my five-year-old son a plastic juicer at her garage sale (piece of junk worth less than a dime) for five dollars. He wanted something for his mom for Mother's Day, sweet + wholesome gesture, but she charged five stinking bucks. He used his saved Tooth Fairy /Christmas / birthday money, but that's not the point right now.

"Mmmhmm," she said. "You think it's computer sex or something? How can we find out? They took him away in cuffs."

"Norma, I have no idea. I'll let you know if I hear anything."

That was one week ago. Since then I've scoured the internet looking for info. Found *nada* til today. Norma wasn't too far off actually. Possession + distribution of child pornography. Also small indoor marijuana growing operation. Hmm, Michael, who knew? Have you ever seen interviews w/ neighbors of serial killers who are in utter shock and say they never saw it coming? "He was a nice guy, quiet, kept to himself." Yeah, well, I saw this one coming a mile away. Michael's a weird son-of-a-bitch. Not shocked at all. But again, he's locked up now. So what great news for you, prospective buyer, knowing that a pedophile's been eradicated from the neighborhood. Thanks to him, I'm lowering price to well-below current market value. My misfortune=your gain. Bad news for me=good news for you.

CL > new river valley > housing > real estate

December 16

House No Longer for Sale (please stop emailing snarky comments)—Nearly Christmas, fed up. Michael incident (see previous post) destroyed property values. Don't know what's wrong w/ you people: couldn't find a better deal if the house smacked you in the face. I've been honest + forthright. Would you rather if I sugarcoated it? Lied? Regardless, house is off market, so please stop bombarding me w/ snide remarks. Especially you, JMV12444355. Up yours buddy. How original: "The whole neighborhood should be firebombed, like they did in Philly that time." That's funny. Know what, JMV12444355? You have no soul. I bet you were adopted. I simply wanted to sell my house. No, check that. Not my house, my *home*. I raised my son here, several dogs, two buried under the pines near the wisteria vine which covers the handmade gazebo. Absolutely gorgeous in spring. The closet door in the extra bedroom chronicles my son's growth, where my wife measured him each year, ever since he was five. His marks are alongside those of the children raised in the house prior, dating back to 1970s, including progression of their son who sadly committed suicide (not inside house, far as I'm aware.) So the home has seen happiness/sadness. It's known anguish + pain, all the while sitting stoically on the hill as its hardwood floors absorbed the tears, it keeping the owners safe + warm + comfortable as best it could. There's the monster oak in the backyard watching over the home, where twice I almost died falling from its branches while building my son's treehouse. Oh, what that tree has seen. Even more than the house, I bet. Maybe it observed Indians (okay, Native Americans) resting under its shade in the now fenced-in backyard. There's a garden + compost pile, also a strawberry patch, asparagus plants. The recycling of life, each + every year. The covering of lettuce + peas w/ tarps when late mountain frosts invade each spring. Do I trust just anyone to mulch my blueberry bushes every autumn? To tenderly care for my babies? Hardly. My home shouldn't be hocked on craigslist just to avoid an agent's 6%. The neighborhood has quirks, yes, but I love it and I'm not leaving. No damn way you'll get me out of here anytime soon. Well, unless the price is right. Drop me a line, let's talk.

CL>new river valley>housing>real estate

July 15

House for Sale by Owner—URGENT—RELISTED—
3br, 1½ bath. Man, life can throw some curveballs, can't
it? Writing this post from Cambridge, Massachusetts.
Wife just landed job at Harvard! Freaking Harvard, can
you believe it? My little rockstar from the Blue Ridge
Mountains, going to the hollowed halls of Harvard.
From Christiansburg to Cambridge. From the poison
ivy to the Ivy League! (I'm being told it's "hallowed"
halls ...my bad.) Outrageous rent up here. 700 sq.
ft. apartment. One month rent = three mortgage
payments back home. Needless to say, house priced
to sell. During month before move, I gutted entire
basement (June, 2015). Fixed flooding problem (see
previous post) which involved heavy duty machinery
including badass concrete saw that will rip through
anything. Spread mortar outside, sealing gaping crack
between foundation + patio. Ripped out water/termite-
damaged wall. You should've seen bonfire I built w/
that discarded paneling in the outdoor fireplace (how
did I not mention this before?—giant stone fireplace,
complete w/grill and spit). Basement masonry block
painted w/10 gallons of DryLock. Goopy, thick shit, let
me tell you. Arms sore as hell. Tore out (asbestos) floor
tile. Used questionable/sketchy/probably illegal disposal
methods. Contemplated the word 'mesothelioma" and
all its potential hazards far more often than I would've
liked. Good news for you, floor no longer a possible
cancer causer. Hung drywall on ceiling, primed/painted
it, mounted fluorescent lights. Place looks amazing. On

night before move, wife absolutely insisted I remove closet door (which chronicled son's height—see previous post) b/c she wanted to take it w/ us to Boston.

"But then the closet won't have a door," I said.

"I...don't...care," she said.

I popped hinges, set heavy son-of-a-bitch on floor, started reading what wife had documented over past sixteen years. Earliest entry was of previous owner's child: Christopher 3'9" 4/9/73 5yrs 11months. Earliest mark for my son: Mason 8/8/99 5yrs 10 months 3'10". One of the final entries read as follows: Mason 8/22/12 (night before leaving for college) 6'4". I must admit, got a little misty eyed. Next day, loaded door on U-Haul. Carefully. Plan: make table out of it, preserving measurements with shellac/veneer/or something. The wife, as usual, made right call. Unbeknown to wife + son, shortly before saying good-bye to beloved house, I entered that door-less closet + wrote a note w/Sharpie on back-facing wall, high up in corner. Who knows if new owners will ever find it? But it might be a cool hidden treasure for someone to discover one day. It read:

We loved this home from 5/98~7/13/2015

We hope you do too!

-The Sanders-

Scott, Jocey, + Mason

LONG ROW TO HOE

Though I didn't know it yet, the teenage boy shuffling across the parking lot had no face. I stood on the concrete front porch of my grandmother's government assisted home, blowing store-bought bubbles for my three-year-old son. Mimi sat in a lawn chair, drinking a beer, watching Mason chase the bubbles, probably as happy as she'd ever been. It was 1996, late spring, humid, with thunderstorms on the prowl. I had made the 500-mile journey from Virginia to the rural town of Wadley, Alabama in order to introduce Mason to Mimi before she died. My last visit had been three years prior for Papa's funeral.

Barely a speck in the eastern part of the state, Wadley was where I'd spent time as a boy on family visits. I fondly recall walking to the five-and-dime for candy or baseball cards, stuffing grass through the chain link fence to feed the neighbor's goat, and fantasizing about catching monster catfish out of the Tallapoosa with Papa. But now the downtown, with its string of brick buildings, was abandoned, save for the grocery store. The hardware store boarded up, the one restaurant closed, the bank, train depot, five-and-dime, all defunct.

As the faceless teenager grew nearer, Mason ran around a tiny plot of grass with his newfound friend, Deon, whose name I knew because his morbidly obese, teenage mother yelled it every few seconds. "Deon, come back here" or "Deon, don't you go too far, boy" or "Deon, I'll whoop your bee-hind." But Deon ignored her and only screamed with delight as he and Mason popped bubbles as fast as I produced them. Deon wasn't being insolent; he was deaf. His mother obviously knew this (it was the first thing she'd told me), yet she continued calling out to him, issuing warnings and idle threats even though Deon couldn't hear one word, had never heard one word. Her commands fell on deaf ears, literally.

Little Deon loved those bubbles. But while he kept running in circles, oblivious, Mason halted when the teenager shuffled closer, zombie-like, making noise with both his mouth and the clicking of his cane, which tapped across the hot macadam as he felt his way forward. In his other hand was a can of beer, a bent straw poking from the top. He wore sneakers and jeans but no shirt, his hair cut short. Mason nudged closer to my leg, wary, recognizing something was off, while Deon looked up at me with confusion and impatience, wondering where the magic bubbles had gone.

A few houses down—I say *houses*, but each residence was connected to the next, creating an elongated, segmented, insect-like chain—a group of teens were partying pretty hard, especially for late afternoon, midweek. Laughing, smoking, drinking beer on their own slab of concrete.

The faceless boy halted in front of us. Maybe he'd heard Deon and Mason squealing, Deon's mother yelling. He raised his beer and with an open mouth, blindly searched for the straw's end like a hungry goldfish. After taking a sip, he yelled, "Going to party, y'all."

Now that he was up close, I inadvertently cringed.

In place of eyes and a nose and lips, there was only a mutilated smudge. As if a circus elephant had taken his hoof and, with one angry swipe, erased the boy's features, leaving behind striated, mangled skin. He didn't wear eyepatches because there were no vacant cavities to hide. Instead, the skin seemed to have melded, forming wrinkled folds over the sockets. I don't recall nostril openings. Though his lips were missing, he could speak, and coherently, though he yelled everything. Whatever had happened to him must have also affected his hearing. My initial guess was burn victim, but his shirt was off, showing a perfectly normal body. A bit of a farmer's tan, his torso thin and wiry, his skin flawless. Only his face had been affected.

Mason clutched my leg and stared. I did the same though every social norm urged me to look away. But the image was so grotesque, so unhuman, it was hard not to gawk. Especially when I was in no danger of being caught. From her lawn chair, Mimi said, "Carl, this is my grandson and great-grandson. They're visiting from Virginia." In any other story involving Mimi, she would've had a cigarette in her hand, a woman who'd smoked several packs a day for sixty-five years. But after Papa died, she'd quit. Unfortunately it was too little too late, as emphysema was already killing her, but I was proud of her all the same. She'd also recently acquired her driver's license thanks to the help of a young black man—early twenties, living across the way with his wheelchair-bound mother, and flamboyantly gay ("I think he might be a bit sweet," Mimi told me when I first arrived)—who'd practiced with my grandmother for months. I thought it was pretty damn cool that this white woman, born and raised in the thick of the segregated South, and a homosexual black man fifty years her junior, were hanging out.

Mimi continued, "They're both standing in front of you, Carl."

"Hey," I said, taking a swig of my own beer, wanting him and his face to go away. His deformities caused me unease, like a visit to a children's hospital. I was awkward, didn't know how to behave.

Carl slurped from his straw. "Come over to the party," he yelled. "We're getting shitty."

I didn't answer straight off, now preoccupied with the clump of gauze protruding from his throat, directly below the Adam's apple, plugging a tracheotomy hole like a loose fitting cork. "We'll see what happens," I said. "Thanks."

"Let's get drunk," he yelled, now directing his words not at me but toward the partiers several doors down.

"Come on over, Carl," voices yelled back, followed by various *woo-hoos* and laughter.

Carl didn't say goodbye, just stumbled off, tapping his cane across the asphalt.

"A few weeks ago," said Mimi, "that boy took a shotgun and tried to blow his head off. Eighteen years old." She didn't bother filtering herself, didn't consider that maybe my son, still clinging sheepishly to my leg, shouldn't hear such things. "Tried to kill himself over a girl. He lives with his mother," she said, indicating a different section of conjoined homes down the hill. "Pretty sure she's on drugs. He's got a long row to hoe."

Mimi wasn't one to get introspective. Things just were the way they were. She'd seen plenty—a child of the Depression, of poverty, of no education, of personal tragedy. Her brother shot himself in the head the night before his wedding. Her only son, my Uncle Walter, died from a pill overdose, possibly a suicide. So some stranger who'd blasted his face off with a shotgun wasn't something she'd be losing any sleep over.

•

When I was ten years old, there was only one person who came close to challenging my father's status of hero. His name was Billy, and he lived up the road in my neighborhood. Fifteen years old, a star wrestler, friendly, considerate, an all-around good guy. "That boy's got a good head on his shoulders," my dad used to say. I was friends with Billy's younger brother, Michael, and was secretly jealous of him for having the big brother I'd always wanted. Billy built snow forts for us in the winter, tree forts in the summer. He taught us how to play Combat on his Atari, spun the latest Billy Joel and Eagles albums on his turntable. He taught us wrestling moves and protected us from the neighborhood bullies. I used to imagine that if something ever happened to Billy's parents, I'd convince my mom and dad to adopt him. Not Michael, just Billy, so I could have him for my very own.

On the evening of May 5th, 1980, red lights flashed through our living room windows. An ambulance and several police cars were parked in Billy's driveway. I notified my mother, who immediately ran out the front door and up the road. Seconds later, the phone rang. It was Billy's mother, crying hysterically.

"Let me speak to your mom."

"She just left for your house," I said. "What's wrong? What happened?"

She hung up.

Mom hadn't returned by bedtime, so Dad pulled me away from the window where I'd been watching the swirling lights—scared, worried, yet thrilled by it all—and tucked me in. The next morning, Mom was at my bedside.

Using a tie, Billy had hanged himself in his bedroom closet. In the same bedroom that he shared with Michael. He left no note, there were no warning signs or indicators. He was gone, and the lives of Michael and his family were shattered. I was also devastated, though too young to fully comprehend it.

Years later, shortly after Michael finished college, his parents sold their house and told him to come by if he wanted to collect any of his old things. While poking around the home, Michael eventually found himself confronted with that bedroom closet—the one he'd done his best to avoid since Billy's death.

When Michael entered, he saw a horizontal bar serving as a coat rack which Billy had used to attach the tie. Opposite that was a shelf, six or seven feet above the floor. Michael noticed some things sitting atop it but couldn't reach them, so he used a plastic milk crate as a stepstool. And it was from this higher vantage point where he observed something pressed into the shelf's soft wood: two sets of elliptical indentions, four small circles to each set. Unmistakably, the marks of Billy's fingers as he'd struggled to get free. A clue hidden for fifteen years.

Based on his findings, Michael now believes Billy was just experimenting with the idea of suicide but got in too deep. Or, once he started the process, he realized he didn't want to go through with it. After he slumped forward, he had tried desperately to push back to a standing position with the aid of the shelf, but his feet couldn't find purchase. He'd wanted to live, he'd fought to survive.

Those hidden marks helped give Michael and his family a bit of solace. A few vague answers to the otherwise unanswerable questions that come with suicide.

•

Here's my theory on Carl's attempt. Much like Billy, he got scared at the very last instant, had second thoughts. He pushed the barrel away at the same moment he squeezed the trigger. If he'd simply left the gun in place, nestled against that soft waddle of skin beneath the chin, the buckshot or birdshot would have acted like a bullet, traveling up through the roof of his mouth and into his brain, having no time to disperse. But if he pushed the gun away, or more likely, pulled his head back as if flinching, it would make sense that the spray would shear off his facial features while missing his brain, sparing his life.

It's also possible he had every intention of going through with it, but simply made a mistake. Using a shotgun would be far more difficult than a handgun because of the long barrel and awkwardness of reaching the trigger. It's feasible the barrel slipped just as he went to squeeze-off the deadly shot.

I'll never know the real circumstances, but of the two scenarios, I'd prefer to believe he got scared at the last millisecond. Realized he wanted to live, the same as Billy.

After the blast, did Carl remain conscious? How long did he lie on the floor, waiting for help? Suddenly blind, his face destroyed, his entire world permanently dark, what sort of pain must he have endured? What thoughts ran through his head?

I know nothing more about Carl, before or after. I'm not even certain I have his name correct. But writing about him, thinking about him, theorizing on his situation, helped resurrect some other distant memories. One had taken place a decade later, when I was picking up a couch from a furniture outlet. I had the truck backed into the warehouse bay, a guy helping me load. He was my age, mid-thirties, jeans and a t-shirt, scraggly hair, a slight paunch. As he fumbled for a solid hold, he kept rubbing his wrist, as if in pain.

"Hurt your hand?" I said, instantly regretting it. One of those times where you feel sick, wishing you could suck your words back in like smoke, swallow them whole. His arm, from the elbow down, was twisted nearly 180 degrees, a complete reversal. His hand was badly mangled—curled and clawed.

"A few years ago," he said, "got drunk with a buddy. Decided to play chicken with a train. The train won." He didn't laugh or smile when he said it, but he didn't act sorry for himself either. He wasn't looking for sympathy. It was matter-of-fact. He'd fucked up and now he owned it, which, in that very brief exchange, I admired.

I wonder if Carl owned it.

I wonder if Carl had one of those "come to Jesus" moments afterward.

Often you hear about suicide survivors who say, "I'm so glad to be alive." I had a friend, Mark, who used a surfboard leash to hang himself in a closet. He'd been twenty years old, his girlfriend had dumped him, and he was well on his way to succeeding in his attempt. By chance, his roommate came home, found him, and saved his life. When he awoke in the hospital, his stepfather sat at his bedside. Mark's first words to him were, "Thank God I'm alive." Twenty years later, however, Mark hanged himself in a different closet. This time he was successful, leaving behind a wife and two boys.

Which makes me wonder about Carl all these years later. Is he still alive? If he was prone to suicide way back then, what must his outlook have been moving forward? Did he wake up after the attempt and say, "Thank God I'm alive" or instead, "Goddamnit, how did I screw this up?"

The repercussions must have been excruciating— tremendous pain and therapy and embarrassment and possible ridicule. Certain humiliation and self-loathing. How many cans of beer with friends would it take to numb all of that? How long until the empathy disappeared, until the friends slipped away, one-by-one, making excuses, ignoring phone calls? When would they eventually find distance, invent distance? They were obligated in the short term, sure, but how long would that loyalty last?

Later that night, at Mimi's house, a tornado warning was issued for east-central Alabama. Rain, wind, thunder, and lightning pounded her little home. As I sat alone on the couch getting drunk, Mimi awoke and shuffled down the hall toward the bathroom. Dressed in a loose nightgown and slippers, she'd always looked the same to me. From the time I was a little boy until the present, she'd always sounded the same, acted the same, looked the same. But on her way back to her bedroom, as she whispered, "Goodnight, Sugar," I was stunned by how old she actually was. She appeared to be an entirely different person, mainly because her lips had caved-in on themselves. It took me a second to understand: she'd removed her dentures. I'd always known she wore them, but I'd never once considered what that actually meant—that she had no teeth, uppers or lowers. In that instant, I realized the true dimensions of her poverty. Realized how elderly she'd become. Realized she didn't have much time left.

As I sat on her couch, getting drunker and drunker, I started feeling sorry for myself, thought about what a fraud I was. In Mimi's eyes, I was the prodigal son. College degree, planned to be an author, had a beautiful wife and child. But in reality I was a loser. I used alcohol to battle my depression. I'd never seriously written a word—an author in fantasy only. Instead, I was a waiter, barely making rent. I was a drunk who still had four years of heavy, hard drinking ahead of me before I'd get sober. I was a father but had no idea what the hell I was doing. Or where I was going. Still as lost as I was at sixteen, but now the stakes were far higher. My own father's oft repeated words taunted me: "When the hell are you going to grow up? You need to get a real job and get your shit together." He was right, and had said these things out of love and concern, but it didn't sting any less.

So I sat there and attempted to suppress his admonitions, his series of rebukes from afar that most often haunted me when inebriated. I tried to avoid dwelling on the upcoming bills I had no money for, lied to myself about how I was fine, how I'd make it big someday. I drunkenly fantasized, for the umpteenth time, about being an author even though I knew it was unattainable. "You can't make money as a writer"— another of my father's harsh proclamations, though he meant "You" in the universal sense, not just me in particular. And regardless of intent, he was once again correct. I wanted the fame and glory but had no concept of the work involved. But I fantasized anyway, knowing that if I ever did become an author, someday I'd write about Billy. I'd write about Carl and Mimi and little Deon. About how one five-minute slot of time so profoundly impacted me.

•

What had Carl looked like before he shot himself? Had he been handsome? Average? Ugly? Everyone who encountered him from that day forward would be disgusted by his appearance—it was impossible not to feel that way—his deformity so extreme that the human brain simply can't process it. He would always be judged as a real-life monster regardless of how kind or gentle or altruistic he might actually have been.

Carl would never know the severity of his disfigurement. He'd be able to use his fingers to probe his face, to gingerly touch where his nose had once been. That might give him a vague idea. But he'd never be able to gaze into a mirror and see what I had seen. In that respect, his blindness might've been a godsend, if only because it spared him from seeing himself. More importantly, it spared him from enduring the reactions of passing strangers.

•

Mimi would die a year later, on my birthday, found by her driving buddy. Sitting in her chair peacefully, the television on, her breath finally having given out. She'd been seventy-eight. Little Deon would be twenty-three by now, same as Mason. What sort of life had he lived? Far different than Mason's, I imagine, who's travelled extensively, who finished sixth in his class and is about to graduate from one of the top architecture colleges in the country. Back then, at the same time Carl shot himself, when I was a drunk and depressed and feeling pretty helpless, my wife Jocey and I were struggling to make ends meet—young parents living in a trailer, collecting food stamps, barely surviving. But we were also privileged. We had education, had parents who'd assist if we asked. They weren't rich, but they had means, which makes a huge difference, just knowing it's there. We had a safety net, which minimized our desperation. I would never know abject poverty the way Mimi had, the way Carl most likely had as he moved forward. I never feared that my family would go hungry, or that Mason couldn't go to the doctor for lack of funds. If worse came to worst, I knew I had backup. Somebody like Carl, on the other hand, didn't have those options, that security.

With tenacity (but mostly because of sobriety) I eventually became a college instructor and a writer. I placed the setting for my first novel in an impoverished town in eastern Alabama. One of the characters was a homeless man, a pariah, who everyone in the town was afraid of. Jocey went back to school in her early thirties to finish the degree she was unable to complete after getting pregnant. She's now employed at Harvard University. She went from living in a trailer in the rural mountains of Virginia to working for the world's foremost institution of higher education. Yo Yo Ma lives around the block from us. Julia Child used to buy her meat at our corner grocery. I occasionally pass the president of Harvard on the sidewalk, another woman from the Virginia mountains who defied all expectations. Two streets over from our apartment, there's an art collector who deals exclusively in Andy Warhol's. That's his job, buying and selling Warhol's original artwork.

I don't belong here.

I'm guessing the art collector and I grew up quite differently. Here's one example of the differences I envision. The first home Jocey and I ever rented, back in 1993, was an old farmhouse, built circa 1845, and located in the heart of the Blue Ridge Mountains. On a dirt road and nestled in a dark hollow, it was the house Mason lived in when he first arrived home from the hospital. We had electricity and water, but no heat, save for a woodstove. No insulation in the walls except for crumpled, decaying newspaper.

Shortly after we moved in, I discovered a snake living in a closet. The woman who'd rented before us hated cats, so she procured a snake to roam freely through the house in order to solve her mouse infestation. Seemed an odd choice to me, but everyone's different, I suppose. Regardless, we weren't informed of this when we moved in, so imagine my surprise when I opened that little door beneath the stairs to find a five-foot blacksnake, coiled and coolly staring back. If Jocey had been the one to open that door instead, I'd be telling a far different story right now. One most likely involving a beautiful young woman who dropped dead of fright way before her time.

After the snake was captured and released in the woods, my inevitable mouse problem quickly intensified. Before long, the little rodents had overrun our cabinets and pantries. Viktor snap-traps were unable to keep pace.

One day I awoke after a night of heavy drinking with nothing to eat but a small Vidalia onion and a can of Campbell's Tomato Soup. I pulled out a skillet, dropped in a pat of butter, started cooking the chopped Vidalia. Once the pieces turned clear, my plan was to add the soup. But halfway through the sautéing, I noticed black spots in the pan. When I examined them closer, the spots were actually pellets of mouse shit.

But I didn't want to waste that onion.

I was hungover and starving, had nothing else to eat, the grocery store was thirty minutes away, and I was broke. So, no, Mr. Art Collector, I didn't throw the contents in the garbage. Instead, I picked out the mouse droppings with a spoon, rinsed off the onion and skillet, and then added that glorious condensed soup from Mr. Warhol's famous can. Then I ate my lunch.

That's the difference between us. You, Mr. Art Collector, acquire paintings of a Campbell's tomato soup can, while I empty an actual one into a pot of onions stained with mouse shit. I'm going to assume you've never done anything like that. Which is a good thing, by the way. I'm the asshole, not you. And this is not something I'm proud of. When my wife reads this, it will be news to her; I'm not anticipating a favorable reaction. Her Harvard colleagues will probably look at me a bit differently now, too. So it goes. I was really hungry, really hungover, and I rolled the dice. Fuck it. I imagine Mimi would understand, had probably been there before. Carl, too.

Sometimes, when Jocey and I are walking the dog around our Cambridge neighborhood, admiring the various multi-million dollar homes we'll never own, most with BMWs or Audis or Porsches in the driveway, some with private ice rinks in the backyard, some designed by the world's most famous architects, some with Warhol originals on the walls (rumor has it), we shake our heads in sincere wonder. We look at each other, chuckle, and say, "How the hell did all this happen?" Sometimes we feel like we don't really belong here. Maybe our humble beginnings are still ingrained in us. I often believe I'd feel far more comfortable in that old farmhouse with my can of tomato soup than I do in our local farm-to-table restaurant eating an $8.95 bowl of tomato bisque.

But don't get me wrong. That doesn't mean the $8.95 bisque isn't absolutely delicious. That doesn't mean we aren't enjoying the ride.

I'm assuming Carl's ride has been far different.

•

What are the chances Carl found a partner who cared for him, who truly loved him, who wasn't physically repulsed? What is the likelihood Carl landed a job? One that offered him purpose. Some sense of fulfillment. What sort of work might a man with no face, with no eyes, be capable of performing?

As much as I'd like to think otherwise, my gut says Carl was probably destined to a life of agony, heartache, government checks, and dependence on his mother. A mother, according to Mimi, who'd already had plenty of problems well before her son pulled that trigger. If I'm correct in those assumptions, then a part of me hopes his suffering ended sooner rather than later, either from natural causes, complications from the shooting, or from his own hand. Similar to my friend Mark, I'm guessing Carl probably finished the job he initially started. And I couldn't blame him for that if he did.

But maybe I'm wrong. Maybe he went on to have a happy and successful life. A productive life. Perhaps he defied all expectations, the same as the president of Harvard, the same as Jocey. Hell, maybe even the same as me in some respects. For Carl's sake, I hope it's true, but man, the odds sure seem stacked against him.

•

I was in elementary school, fifth grade, and we were being shown a film. At the start of the movie, a little boy got hit by a car and was killed, which, in retrospect, was some pretty dark stuff for a bunch of fifth graders. Regardless, an all-consuming depression overtook me. I tried to fight my quivering lip, didn't want to be embarrassed in front of the class, so I bolted for the door. I made it as far as the hallway before I lost it. Started crying uncontrollably. One of those deep, hard cries where you can't even catch your breath. The teacher followed me out, tried to console me, but ultimately my mother was called to come pick me up. I realize now that this happened around the one year anniversary of Billy's suicide. I know this because it was spring, Little League season was in full force, and I had a game later that evening.

I was on the mound, considered one of the best pitchers in the league. But on that night, after my tough day at school, I got shelled. Homerun after homerun. I let up more long-balls in that one game than I did in the rest of my career combined. We lost badly, and afterward I sat on the bench in tears, completely overwhelmed, not even able to get up and shake hands with the other team. Everyone assumed I was upset because of my poor performance, but it wasn't that. Nobody except my parents realized that I was finally grieving for Billy, was still trying to comprehend what the hell had happened. The movie and the game had been catalysts, but not the underlying reasons for my breakdown. It had taken a year for me to escape that fog and finally mourn. Billy's suicide was my "innocence lost" moment, when my worldview shifted, when I learned that life can be brutal. That it doesn't discriminate.

Maybe his death hardened me in some ways. Prepped me for how I would handle all that was still to come, similar to how Mimi's previous tragedies may have contributed to her offhand attitude about Carl. I don't know. But Billy's suicide is something I've thought about often throughout my life, though it has taken thirty-six years to realize I was probably traumatized by it. But back then, I was just a child. I didn't go to a counselor or psychiatrist. I just moved on. That was my only option. My mom talked with me a few times, I didn't say much, I seemed fine, and that was that.

Whatever the case, there's no doubt his death shaped me. Did it lead, in some small way, to my predilection for alcohol, for my future high-risk behavior? I really don't think so. Heredity, it seems, should be more to blame for that. But I'm not looking to place blame, nor am I complaining. I've had a great life. Sure, there were some struggles and sad things along the way, but there were far more happy, fun, and positive things. And who can really say for certain how specific events shape our lives anyway? There's no barometer to gauge all of that. Life just is. My mother and father shaped me, my friends shaped me, New Jersey shaped me. That circus tiger, that molester kid, Carl's disfigurement, Billy's death, they all shaped me. But so did everything else, including what I experienced today. And yesterday. And whatever occurs tomorrow. It's just my life. We all have a story, this one happens to be mine.

Perhaps that's too blasé. Perhaps I'm guilty of that same pervasive don't-sweat-the-small-stuff attitude that most people from New Jersey are known for. For example, when I contacted Nick to get his consent to publish the story about his sons and the heroin, he read the piece and gave it two thumbs up, said it was all accurate. He was pretty nonchalant, especially considering the severity of the material. He texted, "I read it. I'm fine with it. Well written." However, he followed that up in a second text a moment later which encompassed the more infamous Jersey attitude: revenge. "But unlike you, I'm waiting for the day Schmiddy overdoses so I can go piss on his grave."

In Bob Dylan's song *Tangled Up In Blue*, he wrote, "And when finally the bottom fell out, I became withdrawn. The only thing I knew how to do was to keep on keeping on." That feels accurate. That nicely conveys my attitude toward most things. Withdraw, then keep on keeping on. The French have also summed it up pretty well with their eloquent *C'est la vie* to describe those things which are out of our control. *Such is life.*

But people from Jersey also have an expression. Perhaps it's not as clever as Bob Dylan's lyrics or as sophisticated and pleasing to the ear as the French phrase, but it's straightforward and gets right to the point. That's the Jersey way, after all. It's a saying I heard hundreds of times growing up, from my peers, from middle-aged women, from old men smoking cigarettes in the corner booths of pizza places. James Gandolfini, as the iconic Tony Soprano, would often say it, too, generally when dealing with death or some other horrific tragedy. "Ehh, what're'ya gonna do?"

Which sounds about right to me. I think I'll leave it at that.

Some of the essays in this collection were previously published, acknowledged, and/or anthologized, often in slightly different format, in the following publications. "My Father" in *Creative Nonfiction* and later chosen as Notable by *Best American Essays 2015*. "The Second Person" in *Jabberwock Review*. "Circus Prayer" in *Sweet* and later anthologized in *A Book of Uncommon Prayer*. "Cold-Blooded Love" in *Steam Ticket: A Third Coast Review*. "The Lost Art" in *Hippocampus*. A small portion of "Mountain Man" was first published in *Hippocampus* under the title "4/20." "House for Sale by Owner" in *Zone 3*. "Steps" in *Creative Nonfiction*. A small portion of "Long Row To Hoe" was first published in *Spectrum* under the title "A Cross Examination." I thank all of the editors for including my work within their pages.

— *Scott Loring Sanders*

Acknowledgments

I'd like to thank all of the following for their various insights, observations, and suggestions. No matter how big or small, each contributed in their own way, some wittingly, some unwittingly. Matthew Vollmer, who changed my entire mindset with regards to approaching the essay form. It's fair to say this book wouldn't exist without his influence. LauraBess Kenny, my first reader on several of the essays included in this book, and who I depend on greatly in the early stages of a piece. A big thanks to Christine Domas, Laura Platt, Shannon Oldroyd, Angela Mitchell Miss, John F. Borowski, Mark Ligos, Craig Duerr, and Bryan Munnelly for their anecdotes and memories which helped form "The Hookerman's Backyard." I'd also like to acknowledge Betsy Guzenski at the Washington Township Historical Society for her assistance with crime statistics, and the television show "Psychic Investigators" which provided helpful information. A big thank you to the documentary "The Most Insane Waterpark Ever" which provides a hilarious commentary on Action Park and helped me recall some of my own memories. Watch it if you get a chance—you won't be sorry. A shout-out to Michael Reynolds for his friendship and frankness over the years, and also to his book *Surviving Bill*. More shout-outs go to Juges, C&J, Steve Ingersoll, Yim Tan Wong, and my sister, Laura. For early suggestions on the cover, thanks go to Danielle Buynak, Sasha Spriggs, and Mason Sanders. A big thank you to the late Rick Trethewey, who first introduced me to the creative nonfiction genre and encouraged me to keep pursuing it. And lastly, to Jon Roemer, my publisher at Outpost19, who got behind this project early on and showed nothing but enthusiasm, professionalism, and excitement the entire way through. I can't thank him enough.

About the author

Scott Loring Sanders has had short fiction and nonfiction widely published and anthologized, including work selected for *Best American Mystery Stories* and chosen as Notable in *Best American Essays*. Sanders has published two novels, a collection of short fiction, and was the Writer-in-Residence at the Camargo Foundation in Cassis, France. *Surviving Jersey* is his first book of nonfiction.

CPSIA information can be obtained
at www.ICGtesting.com
Printed in the USA
BVOW08s2117100917
494440BV00001B/1/P